HOW TO TELL STORIES

A Latin American Perspective

By Daniel Mato

Translated by Joyce A. Story

© 2020 Daniel Mato

How to Tell Stories: A Latin American Perspective
Written by Daniel Mato
Translated by Joyce A. Story

Under the Stone Publishing
3104 E Camelback Rd #2519
Phoenix AZ 85016 USA

Perfect Bound ISBN: 978-1-947408-26-5

Library of Congress Control Number: 2020916506

ALL RIGHTS RESERVED
No part of this book may be used or reproduced or transmitted in any form or by any means, electronic or mechanical, including photocopying, recording or by any information storage and retrieval system, without permission in writing from the publisher, except in the case of brief quotations embodied in critical articles and reviews.

Cover Art and Photo ©Sol Mato and used with permission.
The background image on the cover is a photo from a fragment of the Mayan Murals of Bonampak.
Interior book design by Medlar Publishing Solutions Pvt Ltd., India

To my mother Arucha,
for having told me stories with gentle kindness.

To my father Rogelio,
for still telling jokes and anecdotes with charm and wit.

To Franciscote and many other folk tellers,
for having generously revealed to me the secrets of their craft.

How to Tell Stories: A Latin American Perspective

CONTENTS

From the Translator   *vii*

To the Readers   *xi*

Introduction   *xiii*

Part One   **How to Tell Stories**   **1**

Chapter One   How to Start   3

Chapter Two   What to Tell: Finding and Selecting Stories   29

Chapter Three   Preparing the Story to Tell   55

Chapter Four   Preparing Yourself to Tell the Story   73

Chapter Five   When and How to Tell   85

Chapter Six   Exercises for Improving Your Telling and for Organizing a Basic Storytelling Workshop   111

Part Two   **Storytelling Applications in the Home and Social Life and in Educational, Social and Cultural Programs**   **121**

Part Three Stories Ready to Tell   **141**

The Mucurutú   143

Won, an Old Tibetan Peasant   150

The Firefly and the Blackberry Bush   154

How Uncle Rabbit Won Aunt Fox's Heart   162

Notes   *173*

Bibliography   *175*

FROM THE TRANSLATOR

Latin America has experienced a resurgence of interest in storytelling, and Daniel Mato has played a major role in this development. His role in the research, dissemination, and revival of storytelling was officially recognized in 2014 at the Nineteenth National Conference on Storytelling in Buenos Aires. Since its appearance in 1994, readers in Latin America have valued his exceptional book *Cómo Contar Cuentos (How to Tell Stories)*, with its dual focus on the art and on the applications of storytelling. The present translation makes Dr. Mato's publication available to the English-speaking world, and the author's insights will be of benefit to all levels of tellers.

Dr. Mato's background and experience render him uniquely qualified to explore the subjects of how to tell stories successfully and how to use storytelling in educational and social settings. His suggestions for developing the ability to tell stories, for example, are shaped by his many years of sharing tales with all types of audiences and conducting scores of storytelling workshops for participants with a wide range of goals. In addition, he has profited from close personal and working relations with indigenous, Afro-descendant, and other Latin American tellers whose storytelling abilities are highly prized in their rural communities. The perceptions gained from this interaction are especially enlightening for readers in the United States as well as in other English-speaking countries. Dr. Mato's contribution to *Traditional Storytelling Today* (1999), edited by the well-known U.S. storyteller and author Margaret Read MacDonald, is an acknowledgment of the value of his findings for readers beyond Latin America. Let us note here that the present translation of Dr. Mato's book offers an extension to the bibliography found in the original publication; these additional research articles underscore the range of Dr. Mato's interest and expertise in the subject of storytelling.

With regard to his understanding of effective applications of storytelling, Dr. Mato is well served by his academic interests and pursuits. Formerly a Social Sciences professor at the Central University of Venezuela, he has also been a visiting professor at several universities in the United States, including Columbia, Dartmouth and New York University, among others. He is considered an expert on cultural diversity, communication, and social change and has frequently chaired or served on research teams that study cultural change in the wake of globalization processes. He currently is Principal Researcher at the National Council of Science and Technology (CONICET) and the National University of Tres de Febrero in Argentina. He also coordinates the project "Cultural Diversity, Interculturality and Higher Education," a program of the International Institute of UNESCO for Higher Education in Latin America and the Caribbean (IESALC).

The remarkable experiences of this storyteller, humanitarian, and internationally known scholar result in an imaginative and, at the same time, solidly practical work. Presented with encouragement, warmth, and humor, Dr. Mato's ideas and recommendations leave his readers eager to explore opportunities for developing their artistic skills, for conducting successful workshops, and for using storytelling in the

From the Translator

home, in educational institutions, and in numerous other professional settings.

As the translator, I wish to dedicate my part in this endeavor to the memory of Dr. Harriet (Betsy) Herlihy, who initiated my interest in storytelling and who supported me at every turn as I pursued the storyteller's path.

Joyce A. Story, Ph.D.

How to Tell Stories: A Latin American Perspective

TO THE READERS

Why tell stories?

There are as many ways to tell a story as there are human beings on the planet Earth to tell them. Those who practice the art of storytelling do so because they enjoy it, and perhaps that is a good reason for you to do it, too. Storytelling is a means of self-expression, of creating, giving, loving, communicating, and sharing with others, and these are always gratifying experiences.

In the home, storytelling serves to strengthen family ties, helping family members to spend more time together and get to know each other better. In the school, storytelling provides another means for communication and for stimulating creative expression. It fosters appreciation of language and literature, and there is no better resource than storytelling for encouraging and developing verbal expression. Storytelling can be a pleasant way to introduce a variety of academic subjects, and it can make daily classes more interesting as well. It is also an excellent resource for libraries to use to encourage reading.

How to Tell Stories

In the most varied kinds of social gatherings, good tellers of anecdotes, jokes, and stories are highly valued for their ability to entertain. With their art, moreover, storytellers can also initiate encounter and exchange among their listeners, facilitate the cohesion of a group or community, assist in defining the group's identity, and foster the group members' awareness of each other's experiences and dreams.

At all times and in all places, the art of storytelling has been an essential part of mankind's experience and cultural expression, and it has enabled human groups to become familiar with, and understand, each other. Today, compelled to consider the humanizing effect of storytelling on our accelerated, technological life, the world is witnessing a rebirth of storytelling in large cities. Every day more and more people are joining this multitude of dreamers who give shape to and share their dreams— the storytellers. Welcome to the sharing of voices, gestures and facial expressions; welcome to the sharing and expanding of dreams.

Daniel Mato

P.S. I would like to know your opinion about this book. In particular, I would like to find out about your experience in utilizing it, what difficulties you have encountered, what was useful and how it was useful.

My email address is: dmato2007@gmail.com

Thank you very much.

INTRODUCTION

The purpose of this book is not to teach my readers to tell stories, but rather to assist them in learning how to tell them.

My goal is to facilitate the learning of some of the techniques and "secrets" of the art of storytelling, and I direct my book particularly to those who haven't had either the opportunity to become skilled in this art in the traditional way—that is, by systematically observing other tellers for several years—or the chance to participate in storytelling courses and workshops. The book can also serve as a memory aid and guide not only for those who are already storytellers or who have, at the very least, participated in a workshop and who wish to increase their knowledge and skills, but also for schoolteachers and professors of language, literature and theater who are seeking ways to motivate their students.

The book is designed to satisfy the needs of parents, teachers, professors, actors, announcers, masters of ceremony, social workers, professional people whose work calls for interpersonal interaction, community group members, and people who simply wish to tell stories to their friends. Those who choose to dedicate themselves professionally to the art of storytelling will also find a way to get started in the profession as well as some exercises they can integrate into their practice. Nonetheless, they will have to dedicate time to developing their expressiveness and creativity not only through workshops but also, and especially, through the traditional forms of learning this art, a fact which presupposes, as with any other art, years of dedication.

My book is divided into three parts. The first chapter of Part One offers a panorama of the art of storytelling in various times and cultures. The chapters that follow present a method of self-learning based on exercises that are easy to do and that will allow readers to move forward in their learning process in keeping with their own interests and abilities. Finally, there are suggestions concerning how and when to tell a story and how to use puppets, music, and other ancillary materials in storytelling; some additional exercises are offered for improving one's own telling and for helping to familiarize others with this art. In Part Two, various practical applications are proposed for the home, the school, entertainment programs, and other professional fields. Part Three presents stories that are ready to tell. Lastly, the Bibliography offers additional sources for those who wish to investigate a given subject more fully.

This book is the result of various experiences. It is above all a re-working and expansion of a workbook published in 1987 and of a series of articles appearing in the journal *Estampas* in Caracas in 1986 and then reproduced in various Latin American publications. It also benefits from the workshops I have facilitated for some two thousand people in various Latin American and Caribbean countries for the past seven years. In addition, I have spent several years visiting peasant and indigenous tellers in various regions of Venezuela, sharing endless storytelling sessions with them, observing their art, and questioning them about how they learned their craft. Finally, I have reflected on all of these experiences and on my own performance as a teller.

PART ONE

HOW TO TELL STORIES

How to Tell Stories: A Latin American Perspective

CHAPTER ONE

HOW TO START

Learning to Tell a Story

Telling stories (tales, legends, sagas, anecdotes, jokes and the like) is one of the oldest forms of creative expression in human history, and we find variations of it in all cultures on our planet. Countless people have cultivated storytelling, but their listeners have always made a distinction between good and bad tellers. Whatever their language, listeners say that good storytellers "know how to tell" and are captivating, full of life, charismatic, and stimulating.

When you speak with these privileged individuals, the good storytellers, you discover that with few exceptions they don't think that they were born with a special talent. They usually say that they have developed their art little by little, observing the best tellers in their family or community for years. They also say that at the same time that they were observing and learning the good teller's resources and secrets, they were putting them into practice by telling stories for community members, relatives, and friends.

That is precisely the reason why these pages weren't conceived to teach you to tell, but rather to help you learn to tell, because your becoming skilled at storytelling depends above all on you—on your own ability to observe and then apply what you have observed. What this book can do is propose exercises for guiding and enhancing your abilities for observation and application so that what would otherwise take you years to accomplish will take far less time.

Stop to observe a friend who is really involved in telling you about something unusual, something different from the ordinary, such as a trip, an automobile accident, an amusing mishap or a child's prank. You will see that he is "telling" just as you or I do several times a day, and, in the final analysis, just as professional tellers do when they are standing before an audience. In reality, we all know how to tell, and we are all used to telling; it is on this basis of prior knowledge and experience that you can learn to tell better and heighten your appeal as a storyteller.

The first step is to realize that when you tell some friends about an accident on the corner and when a teller tells a magical tale for hundreds of spectators, in a certain sense you are both performing the same kinds of actions. Those of the storyteller may have some special appeal for his audience, but when you are relating any event from daily life that is to some degree unusual, you are putting into play the same personal resources that a skilled teller does: the ability to evoke an event and tell it in an organized way, using words, tone of voice, gestures and other resources that we will identify later.

Basically, you have the same abilities as a professional storyteller. If you want to tell better, you have to develop your own abilities and not imitate another teller in any way. Just as each age and each culture have their own forms for manifesting a given art, so each individual develops his own style. And the development of one's own style is precisely what this book will give priority to.

To be initiated into the art of storytelling, therefore, you must understand that the widespread image of an old woman seated in a rocking chair before a group of children is only one example and not the model par excellence. So, if you aren't particularly old and don't have a rocking chair, you don't need to worry; nor should you be worried if both situations do apply to you. As with any art, you must find your own style, and for that, the only limits are your imagination and your creative potential.

In order to develop your personal style, you must observe yourself as well as your surroundings. Becoming familiar with the different ways that stories are told in other cultures in the world, however, will be both useful and interesting. You will see that there many ways to tell stories and that they differ from one people to another, from one teller to another and, for the same teller, from one occasion to another as well.

It is likely that for now you don't have the time or the money to take a world tour. Don't worry; I'll help you solve the problem. I invite you to accompany me in the next pages on a voyage around the planet to observe storytellers in action. This imaginary trip will have several advantages: you won't need to move from your chair or pay for airplane tickets or hotels, and you will even be able to visit some tellers from the past. What do you think? Are you coming with me?

World Tour of Storytellers in Action

Oceania. Several years ago, in the Trobriand Islands to the northwest of New Guinea, the anthropologist Bronislaw Malinowski observed the native custom of meeting at dusk to tell *kwkwanebu*, or "fairy tales." He commented in his writings that when the teller was performing his role in the right way, he elicited laughter, responses, and interruptions from his audience. Malinowski also said that each story, although known by many, could only be told by its "owner"; the latter could teach it to others, however, and authorize them to tell it (1985:115).

The renowned anthropologist stated that:

> ... not all the "owners" know how to evoke the warm laughter that is one of the principal purposes of the tales. A good teller has to change his voice in the dialogues, sing the songs with the necessary emotion, gesticulate and, in general, perform before the audience. Some of the stories are in reality extremely vulgar jokes; others are not [...] (Malinowski 1985: 115–116).

His commentary is very interesting because it demonstrates that sometimes what matters is not the content of the story but rather the manner of telling it.

In Trobriand, as in most of the world, a good storyteller is expected to have in his arsenal of skills the ability to change his voice in dialogues and to portray the characters in his story.

Asia. In seventeenth century China there lived a storyteller so extraordinary that he was called the "king of the Chinese tellers." Fortunately, I was able to find a testimony to his manner of telling:

> [When Liu Jinting tells,] his voice goes from a thundering bellow to a melodious murmur; his expression goes from one of tears to one of laughter. The traits, the voices, the behavior and the gestures of each character are portrayed so vividly that the audience has the sensation of being in the story alongside the characters, while the teller seems to disappear from the scene (Zhenren 28).

Again, we see the importance of expressiveness of voice and the value that is placed on change of voice and on character portrayal. Moreover, just as we saw when we were flying over Oceania, the Chinese tellers have always maintained that a good teller can turn a bad story into something extraordinary and that, on the contrary, an unskilled teller can ruin a good one (Hrdlickova 171).

Let's go to Japan, where there are two principal kinds of storytelling: *Rakugo* and *Kodan*. Both are practiced regularly and are very popular; indeed, in Tokyo the tellers are featured in halls specially prepared for their art, and there are also tellers who perform on radio, on television, and in entertainment spots, including night clubs.

Rakugo consists of humorous stories that last between ten and twenty minutes. Dialogue is more prominent than direct narration. The *rakugoka*, as the tellers of *Rakugo* are called, use a fan and a handkerchief to represent various objects (a sword, a stick for carrying a load on their shoulder, a book, or a bottle, for example.). The use of these items presupposes a display of gestures and facial expressions so rich that the audience is made to believe that the objects represented are actually in the teller's possession (Hrdlickova 176–178).

The way the artists act on stage is so natural and spontaneous that they seem to be speaking to a small circle of friends. In fact, it is the tellers' custom to converse with their audience, who, moreover, usually drink green tea before, during, and after each telling. When tellers begin their performance, they introduce themselves and talk about the weather, customs, or some other subject, and they tell jokes as well; then they introduce the story and begin to tell it (Hrdlickova 176–179).

The tellers are at all times kneeling on a cushion, in the Japanese fashion, and from there they carry out all their movements and dramatizations. Their body expression, therefore, is concentrated in the face, arms, hands and torso. In order to indicate the characters of the dialogues, they use the position of their bodies and turn their heads from one side to the other. When they go from one character to another, they pause briefly and establish direct visual contact with the audience; their gaze is firm and focused. They also look directly at the audience to signal the transition from dialogue to direct narration (Hrdlickova 180).

Kodan consists of extensive tales on historical themes; most often they have a moralistic tone that generally attracts an older audience. These stories are told day after day through episodes lasting from thirty minutes to an hour. The atmosphere is more intimate than in *Rakugo*, and the listeners even lie down on the floor, drink green tea, and eat. The *kodanshi* tell kneeling down, behind a low table. In *Kodan*, the language is more flowery and is richer in archaic words, and there are more descriptive passages and direct narration than dialogue (Hrdlickova 185–186).

The *kodanshi* also have techniques for winning the audience's support and interest, such as inserting news and episodes from modern life into their historical narrations. When the story is divided into episodes, as is most often the case, they usually give a quick summary of what happened in the preceding episode before they begin their telling for the day. The *kodanshi* gesticulate less and tell more slowly than the *rakugoka*. They use a fan and a bamboo pole, and they bang the pole on the table to get the audience's attention and to mark important points of the story (Hrdlickova 186–188).

Europe. Storytelling not only occurred in the past among Europeans, but, as we see from the following passage, it is still practiced today and not just in homes, schools and libraries but in other professional fields as well:

> During Christmas of 1982 storytelling events in three municipalities of Val-du-Marne 'demonstrated once again the current passion for this genre. The term passion is not exaggerated, for all three events involved a large, enthusiastic, and in part proselytizing audience,' which

included not only children but many adults as well (Colombier 37–39).

This is merely one testimony to the current revival of the art of storytelling in France, where there are several regional organizations of tellers and more than fifty professional storytellers in various "modern" cities. Many tellers accompany themselves on a musical instrument or use puppets and techniques of mime and theater in their performances.

I remember with special nostalgia a Halloween night in the south of England in the year 1977. I was seated in a countryside pub talking with some friends when a man dressed in black entered, glancing around furtively and carrying an old candelabra in his right hand. With his left arm he pressed a huge, dusty old book against his chest. He went up to the bar and then went around to the other side. Suddenly the lights went out. The man put the candelabra on the counter, lit the candles one by one, shook the dust off from the book, and began reading a story about a headless horseman. Little by little he looked away from the book, directing his gestures and his eyes, gleaming in the candlelight, toward those present. The pub was frozen in silence; all of us were captivated by the magic of that storyteller. He continued telling in this fashion for about an hour, one story after another. Suddenly he blew out the candles and disappeared. At that time, I was telling stories only to my daughter and her friends. This experience in the English pub opened new horizons for me as a storyteller.

With respect to earlier times in Europe, we turn to Paul Sebillot's preface to a collection of stories told by Breton sailors at the end of the nineteenth century. The renowned researcher stated that for several weeks the sailors gathered around those who were known as good tellers in order to share tales of magic, diabolical adventures, and funny stories. There were tellers so extraordinary that their listeners seemed at times to believe that they were indeed present at the events narrated; one could even hear exclamations of admiration for the beauty of a princess. The interaction between the teller and the audience was, according to Sebillot, an important aspect of each telling (Sebillot 1882: V-XII). It was not only sailors who frequently told stories at that time, but also mothers, wet nurses, peasants, woodsmen and others, and there were tremendous differences in how the stories were told (Sebillot 1913: 15–2 [sic]).

Sometimes the teller encouraged audience involvement either by directly asking his listeners questions about events as he recounted them or by beginning with a formula that became a game of vocal interaction known to the listeners and calling for their participation. Among the sailors, for example, the teller would say "Crick," and the audience would respond "Crack," and this exchange would be repeated over and over and more and more loudly until the group ended up laughing. The teller would then begin his story in this participatory atmosphere (Sebillot 1913: 20–24). The "Crick-Crack" formula, as we will see later, has also been observed among some natives of North America and on various islands of the Caribbean, and today it precedes the telling of stories about Anansi, the mischievous Brother Spider of the *Ashanti* tradition.

Africa. After a lengthy study, Sebillot made the following generalization about storytelling in both Europe and in Africa:

> There are tellers who take great interest in their story, vary their intonation, liven up the dialogue, and, like actors, try to adopt a tone suitable to the various characters that are speaking. I have known women and sailors, for example, who in the case of the Jaguins' comical stories, which are almost completely in dialogue, achieved such effects of comic diction that a professional actor would have envied them. Some were so carried away by their own telling that they seemed personally involved in the

heroes' adventures and spoke as if they could actually see them (Sebillot 1913:19).

Storytellers are still very important in various African cultures. Fernando Ortiz, the well-known researcher of the African presence in the Americas, maintains that:

> There is no person more popular among Africans than a good storyteller [...]. Sometimes the telling occurs in the middle of the square with all the inhabitants seated on the ground opposite the teller [...]. Frequently the teller interrupts his recitation by breaking into song, and the audience repeats it over and over in a singsong voice until the teller is ready to tell a new episode (Ortiz 422–23).

He also affirms that the African tellers

> use very expressive pantomime in their descriptions, and the audience is kept in suspense even if the stories are already well known and the teller's abilities to mimic are widely recognized. All the events of the story are reproduced with parody and are accented with onomatopoeic expressions [...]. Some historians declaim their epics to the rhythm of a drumbeat with which the tellers interweave the melodies of their recitation (Ortiz 423).

There are some storytellers who make use of pantomime and singing skills or are accompanied by instruments and encourage audience participation. The same Ortiz informs us, moreover, that when the Ibos of Nigeria tell stories, it is their custom to portray every type of animal, imitating their voices and typical movements (Ortiz 408). Ortiz also says that among the Bantus, storytellers are very famous for their mannerisms, mimicry, body expression, and ability to imitate the voices of children, the elderly, and other characters as well (Ortiz 424). Naturally, there are differences in quality:

> As you can easily imagine, not all storytellers and mimes give brilliant performances. In Africa, as in the rest of humanity, genius is exceptional […]. Some of the beginning tellers are unimpressive, slow, and tedious, and they confuse the episodes […]. But others are full of life, and one experiences true literary enjoyment upon hearing them […] (Ortiz 423).

The Americas. Live storytelling was an important activity in various indigenous cultures in the Americas before the arrival of the Europeans and the Africans.

The figure of the storyteller, for example, existed among the Nahuatl of Mexico. A codex of the time describes the ideal figure of the "*tlaquetzqui*, who makes things come to life when he speaks." León-Portilla transcribes a text taken from Folio 22 of the Matritense Codex of the Royal Academy that says:

> The teller:
> elegant, captivating
> when he speaks, artist of
> the lip and the mouth.
>
> The good teller:
> he has on his lips
> flowers of *pleasing* words, of happy words.
> In his speech stories abound,
> flowers of the correct word burst from his mouth.

His speech is pleasing and happy like flowers;
His language is noble and his expression refined.

The bad teller:
Broken language,
He tramples on the words;
He bites his lip, speaks badly;
He tells things foolishly, he describes them dryly,
He says vain words,
He has no shame.

(León-Portilla XXXIXXXI)

This testimony needs no further comment: it shows not only the existence of the figure of the storyteller but also the importance accorded to the words he chose and how he said them.

Later, with the conquest and colonization of the Americas, the interaction between European, African and American cultures and, in the Caribbean, Asian culture as well, resulted in the development of many different approaches to storytelling.

Besides the "traditional" teller whose activity is limited to small social spheres, today another type of teller has come into being in many major cities, one whose style is more adapted to "modern" urban life and whose repertory is based more on systematic bibliographical searches than on learning through the oral tradition. This movement of rebirth in the art of storytelling is now taking place in various countries of the Americas, such as Argentina, Bolivia, Brazil, Cuba, Mexico, Venezuela, Uruguay and the United States.

In the United States, for example, there is an extensive, organized movement of storytellers that includes more than three hundred professionals and that organizes some sixty festivals a year. Some of the festivals take place in large areas and use amplifying equipment, while others occur in small groups; sometimes the tellers incorporate theatrical elements such as costumes and stage design with experimental zeal (NAPPS, 1988). *[Translator's Note 1]*

But the urban revival of this art coexists with its traditional forms:

> […] one evening […] stories are told in a small village in the West Indies. The location is the hut of a member of the community, in front of which the teller and his audience, many of them children, are seated around the faint light of a lamp or are illuminated by the light of the moon. The leader of the ritual begins the "Crick-Crack" formula, and he signals to some member of the group who tosses out a riddle […] The session begins on a merry note […] As the story advances, the teller acts out each detail of the plot. His voice is high and whining when the swindler is in a difficult situation and begs for help; it is serious when the victor speaks of a battle. The members of the audience, with their shining eyes fixed on him, are more than listeners. They interrupt the story with exclamations, and when the teller occasionally inserts a song sung by one of the characters, the audience fully participates in the singing, becoming the teller's chorus (Herskovits 1981: 470–471).

In the United States, there are tellers of many different personal styles and of various ethnic and social origins. There are even testimonies that President Abraham Lincoln was famous in the White House for his talent for telling. He used to tell stories while reclining in his chair with his long legs stretched out toward the chimney. He mimicked characters and portrayed scenes by imitating sounds and voices and gesturing with his arms and legs, and his melancholy face was notably animated. His look, his laughter, the slapping of his legs—his whole expression—recalled the storytelling style characteristic of small, Midwestern country towns (Dorson 298).

In Mexico, the art of storytelling that was cultivated among indigenous and peasant groups is also now experiencing an important revitalization in the cities. In 1985, under the guidance of the writer and storyteller Eduardo Robles Boza, the National Association of Storytellers was created ("Crean Asociación" 2–3). Since then, this association has carried out its work in the Chapultepec Forest in Mexico City and in other urban areas, telling stories to all kinds of audiences, especially children. It recently organized a Latin American Storytelling Festival.

In the Caribbean, the panorama of oral narration is richly diverse. In St. Vincent, for example, the custom of telling the stories of Anansi, "Nansi stories," is preserved, generally in places such as bars and corners where men meet, but it is especially prevalent at wakes after the first night. These tales are told in a markedly different way from the style used for other stories. The teller is expected to act out a good part of the actions that make up the story, to imitate the characters' voices, and to create a boisterous mood. In keeping with Anansi's character, the teller assumes the manner of a mischievous trickster, and he plays with it to create a certain atmosphere in the audience. Normally he starts by saying "Crick-Crack," to which the audience responds, "Rockland come!" Accompanied by the clapping of hands, this interaction grows faster in rhythm and rises in volume until the teller starts his story, which generally includes circle dances and songs (Abrahams 168–186).

In Cuba, aside from the "traditional" tellers who perform in smaller social spheres, the poet Eliseo Diego promoted an important storytelling movement from the José Martí National Library beginning in 1966. What is most interesting here is that in order to support the movement, the library began publishing a collection of texts for tellers, probably the first of its kind in Latin America. Although the collection basically aspires to use storytelling to encourage children to read, it nonetheless points out that storytelling is "a manifestation of the Fine Arts." Indeed, the movement has had its effect beyond libraries: "Among enthusiasts there is a movement of storytellers who, though small in number, are already seeing encouraging results" (Broderman 8). Recently the Cuban tellers Miriam Broderman and Garzón Céspedes traveled to other Latin American countries with their art.

In Belize, audience participation in storytelling occurs much more frequently than in other Caribbean cultures. The favorite stories are also those of Anansi; as in St. Vincent, they usually begin with the "Crick-Crack" formula. Interruptions are viewed very favorably as an opportunity not only for the audience to participate but also for the teller to test his skill in picking up the story thread again. Frequently the story includes group songs. When telling is done in the round, the audience also stands up to dance, and the teller signals various members of the audience to go to the center of the circle and do character imitations (Beck 417–34).

In Panama, among the Cuna of the San Blas archipelago, there are two forms of sharing stories: telling them and singing them. In addition to the audience, two people are needed when a story is told. One does the telling, and the other asks questions and makes comments, generally with humorous intent. The teller speaks in everyday language, varying his rhythm and volume and imitating voices and sounds in order to provoke laughter. When the story is sung, two people are also necessary. The second person's interventions do not occur randomly, however, but rather follow a pre-established rhythm, and his language, less everyday in nature, is richer in metaphors (Sherzer 145–163).

In Bolivia, many indigenous communities preserve the practice of storytelling (Jemio). In my travels I heard repeatedly about an *iatiri* whose representations of a story's characters were especially convincing; his manner of portraying a condor by letting his poncho blow in the wind was particularly noted. In 1988, Pia Córdova, of the Venezuelan group TAPICNO, and I offered a workshop in the city of La Paz; it facilitated the formation of a group of urban tellers who intend to turn to their own roots and revitalize the art of storytelling ("Se Realiza Taller" 1).

In the far south of the continent, in Patagonia and Tierra del Fuego, it was the practice of the Selkman Indians to tell stories while seated around a fire. Many personal experiences were recounted, and the event included the interventions of skilled listeners. Somewhat to the north, in Chaco, on Argentine territory, the Mataco also include in their storytelling the interventions of people who are skillful at it (Wilbert and Simoneau 17–18).

In Argentina in 1965, the Storytellers' Club of the Summa Institute was founded in the city of Buenos Aires. Encouraged by Professors Marta Salaotti and Dora Pastoriza de Etchebarne, the Institute had already begun some informal activities in 1960. With time, their courses have led to the creation of similar groups in the interior of Argentina and also in the city of Montevideo, Uruguay. As a rule, the women in these clubs are teachers, and they usually tell their stories to children while seated (Maunas 46–47). More recently, some workshops I coordinated in the cities of Buenos Aires, Córdoba, Neuquón, and Rosario helped to foster the formation of several groups of storytellers. Most of them work with both children and adults. They generally stand while telling and use rich gestural and vocal techniques (Cordova 33).

Meanwhile, Brazil has witnessed an urban rebirth of this art, and in 1978 the First Paraíba Storytellers' Day took place in Paraíba. Many of the tellers were domestic servants and manual laborers. Some documents of the event included descriptions of the performances, and we learn that many of the tellers were especially notable for their expressiveness, particularly their gestures and voice variation (NUPPO).

Venezuela. I have been able to study the art of storytelling more thoroughly in my own nation, both from traveling about the country and from visiting libraries. No matter where you live, therefore, it would be useful for you to join me in this somewhat more detailed leg of our journey. You will see how even within the same country, there are many different forms of storytelling.

Among the indigenous ethnic groups of Venezuela, the forms of telling vary greatly. Let's look at some cases that have already been studied.

The renowned researcher Johannes Wilbert notes that among the Waraos, the teller or "owner of the stories," called *denobo arotu*, is usually an adult male who has good diction and can express himself vividly. It is not unusual, however, to hear a young man tell a story with great talent. Wilbert says the following about his experience among the Waraos:

> Facial expressions, movements of the torso, and waving the arms and hands are dramatic methods that the teller commonly employs. He snaps his fingers to denote something pleasant. The repetition of words in a slow, piercing voice indicates distance, height, and magnitude. A very common and effective strategy for gaining time is to begin a sentence with the gerund of the last verb in the preceding sentence. Groans and whistles are also frequently used (Wilbert n.d.: 15–16).

With regard to the Pemon Indians, Fray Cesáreo de Armellada, who lived among them for a long time and collected many of their stories, maintains that:

> In addition to the many interjections, which I found untranslatable, the telling involved such imitation of voices, gestures, stances, and other declamatory devices

that it was almost the equivalent of a stage presentation (Armellada 10).

The famous anthropologist Marc de Vivrieux (10) tells us that:

> Each "owner of stories" *(makiritare)* leaves the mark of his style and personality on the stories he tells [...]. Each version brings the story into focus in its own way and is distinctive for its silences, for what it leaves to be inferred and what it states outright. It has its own system of incomplete references in keeping with the moment and the mood of the teller and the listeners.

The film *The Initiation of a Shaman*, directed by Manuel De Pedro, has some images of shamans *(yanomami)* telling stories outside of ritual time and space to a group of children. It allows us to appreciate how the rich, expressive and complex gestures and imitation of sounds that characterize their manner of telling is appropriate not only for the ritual space of an initiation ceremony but also for the ordinary telling of a story to a group of children. To directly observe this type of telling one can turn to relevant images in the film, but the following testimony can also be illustrative:

> The mythology recounted by the great shamans is sheer performance. A circle is formed around the "actor"— the man in a trance—by the "spectators," who are never passive; the communication and exchanges among them are constant. At the very least each of them knows the plot of the story, which they comment on as it is being told. One cannot help but recall Artaud's concept of the theater. Scenes which cannot be repeated in our society today but which were not totally ignored in the

past [...]. The elements of dramatic play are part of the Indian's cultural universe [...] it is not solely the shaman who participates in the drama, [...] a close affinity, almost a complicity, is established between him and each spectator, who thus intimately and personally feels the message of the story unfolding before him (Lizot 7–8).

In addition to information from documents, I can turn to some personal experiences. I have had the opportunity to share endless tellings of stories, anecdotes, jokes and legends in various communities, villages, and cities in the interior of Venezuela and to observe from very close up the art of more than fifty traditional tellers and of various professionals as well. I can verify, therefore, that the forms of telling vary quite a bit not only from region to region, but also from teller to teller, and even the same teller can narrate the same story in many different ways on different occasions.

Among the indigenous Guayúu of the state of Zuli, it is not gesture and look that are most important in their *jaiechi* (extensive stories that are sung) but rather the countless tones of voice that embellish the story. Guillermo Uriana, for example, tells in this fashion. Menejo, another Guayúu teller, never loses the opportunity to portray his characters, and he constantly interacts with his audience. Both tellers tend to use objects they find on hand to enrich their stories. During their telling, as in the telling of any of the Guayúu, there is extensive and active audience participation with questions, marginal comments, and jokes addressed to the teller. The Kariñas of the state of Anzoátegui tell their stories in different ways. As a rule, the young teller Neptalí is careful to portray all the characters in his stories. The older tellers, however, rarely even extend an arm to indicate the course of the adventures unfolding in the story.

Among the peasant tellers one should mention Franciscote, a teller from the state of Miranda who is nearly 70 years old. When he is in front of his audience, he is like a playful child. He can throw himself down on the ground to portray a feeble man caught under the paws of a tiger; he can jump, wave his arms like wings, and imitate bird calls to convey the passing of a flock of birds; he can sing a beautiful song each time the hero of the story must call his faithful dogs Onza, Tiger, and León; he is likely to take a shirt or a plastic bag in order to quickly fabricate a "crown" and personify a king. He can draw a large audience into a horror story with his voice, and he can also provoke laughter with his mischievousness in humorous stories, all the while effectively interacting with each listener present.

José Miguel Uzcátegui is an Andean teller full of surprises. In ordinary conversation he is noticeably timid, and it is hard for him to find the right words to express himself. As soon as he begins to tell, however, he is different person; his voice is assured and engaging, he becomes amazingly fluent, and he gives way to a rush of emotions. Making use of his entire body and of objects he finds on hand, José Miguel imparts all these qualities to his audience, representing kings, fairies, and princesses with absolute conviction. The Andean tellers Mano Chico and Mano Cola are also outstanding; both are old, slow, and careful in speech, and they use infrequent and controlled gestures as counterpoint to their stories. One of them tells stories of fairies and spells, while the other tells of priests and saints. In the same region, Oliva Torres is striking for her unusual energy and expressive power in telling all kinds of stories, including tales of fairies and spells, jokes, and dreams. She assumes the role of many different characters and moves about over a large space while performing her actions.

Cheguaco is an outstanding storyteller on Margarita Island. He is masterful in his relations with his audience and can take advantage of any situation that comes up to make it a part of his story. Cheguaco's gestures and facial expressions are rich and varied. Bertha Vargas, a teller from the state of Sucre, now rarely tells stories at wakes as she did until a few years ago, but when she does, she stands and mischievously imitates each of the characters with her unique way of walking and with her expressive voice. When she tells old tales of magic to her grandchildren, on the other hand, she is seated and uses little body movement; with intense gestures and facial expressions, however, she incorporates a song into each story, and the low, deep voice of this old black woman gives her listeners goosebumps.

Lorenzo tells stories in the plains of Guárico with extraordinary body movement, and he directly involves his listeners in his stories by using them to represent characters and objects. He utilizes chance objects on hand to complement his tales as well. The brothers Coronado, in the state of Sucre, also have a marked tendency to incorporate a variety of objects into their telling.

Luis Ramón Márquez, in the state of Portuguesa, is the only full-time professional teller I have known. He has made several recordings, has a show that he has presented in several Argentine cities, and is a convinced and convincing defender of the artistry of storytelling. In his detailed story about the plainsman who came to Caracas one day when there was a baseball game and who ended up in the stadium extremely confused, Marquez portrays five characters in different places on the stage; he passes from one interpretation to the other without any lapses whatsoever. In the meantime, he imitates the sounds of the game and of the crowd.

There have been three festivals in Caracas in recent years, and they revealed very different styles of storytelling. Rafael Rivero Oramas, the legendary storyteller of radio popularly known as Uncle Nicholas (Tío Nicolás), is almost eighty years old; he used to tell stories to a small group of friends in his house, using a rich variety of gestures and imitating all sorts of sounds. The no less legendary Luis Luksic, as a result of his health problems, told with few gestures but with rich imagination and emotion.

Blanca Graciela Arias de Caballero, with her head of gray hair and her distinguished demeanor, does not hesitate to portray Uncle Rabbit (Brer Rabbit, as he is called in the United States) when he is caught by his feet and hands by the doll made of tar. She usually does this seated in a chair with her arms and legs stretched out, imitating the rabbit's plea for help in a lively voice. Meanwhile, dozens of younger tellers have become special kinds of enthusiasts, many of whom dedicate many hours a week to the art of storytelling. One can see different styles, repertoires and conceptions in these young tellers. In the group TAPNICO, for example, we have been developing two storytelling styles simultaneously, depending on the circumstances and the staging areas in which we offer our production. One of these styles rests wholly on the figure of the individual teller, who essentially portrays his characters through voice and gestures, without the aid of any objects. The other style of telling consists of more complex performances, like "The Return of Uncle Rabbit" and "Fantastic Beings of the Caribbean," where we have tried to use a variety of objects and masks, specially produced puppets of different types and sizes, and the incorporation of song. Both styles comply with our interest in experimenting with the different approaches of the "traditional form" as well as the new dimension of the "urban creators." In both instances we try to develop what we have observed in our travels among small villages and communities. We are seeking expressive creative alternatives for developing a unique manner of telling.

Storytellers' Actions and Personal Abilities

As the preceding overview demonstrates, there is no single way to tell a story, and each person must develop his own style. The overview also allows us to note that just like any individual who tells a story, professional tellers make use of words—not written words, however, but words that take shape in the voice. The tellers also make use of body expression, looks, and interaction with those present. They can portray characters, perhaps move about in space, and make use of helpful objects as well.

That is what tellers do that the audience can readily perceive. In addition, however, everyone who decides to tell a story, whether a professional or not, engages in certain other procedures, some more conscious than others: he selects the story (tale, anecdote, legend, for example); he consciously structures its events and at the same time evokes the images and emotions that fit them; and, lastly, he imaginatively re-creates the events in order to convey them to his audience.

It can be said that storytellers apply various personal abilities to perform a number of actions. Let's represent this process as follows:

1) they select the story
2) they structure the story
3) they evoke and imaginatively re-create the actions to be narrated and the circumstances in which the actions take place
4) they share the story with an audience, relying on such resources as:
    - their language (the words and how they are combined)
    - their voice expression
    - their gestures or expression with the body (including looks)
    - their ability to interact with the audience
    - their ability to portray characters
    - their ability to use space effectively
    - their ability to use of objects as symbolic images.

These are the resources, given here in abbreviated form, which tellers put into play. You are undoubtedly aware of many of them and use them more or less on a daily basis. Even if you aren't aware of utilizing all of them, particularly the last three, you probably have used them at some point.

Haven't you ever made fun of a friend's, relative's, or fellow worker's manner of walking, standing up, falling, or running? Try to remember. If memory fails you here, then go back to your childhood. Think back to when you used to play at being a pirate, a cowboy, a doctor, a teacher, or a mom or a dad. Do you see that you, too, can portray characters? Haven't you ever made use of space in those games? Haven't you ever shown your interest or disinterest in a person or an event by drawing closer or by taking a step back? Come on now … you should at least remember some amorous situation. Do you see that you, too, can make meaningful use of space? And what about your extraordinary ability to use objects in a symbolic way? I am sure that on more than one occasion in your childhood games you held a stick or a pencil to represent a gun, or you used a chair to represent a car, an airplane, or a boat, or you made use of a wall to represent a blackboard or a broom to represent a horse. Surely you have done the same thing while telling (note that I use the word "telling") about a traffic accident, for example, and drawing on whatever objects were at hand to show how the vehicles collided and were knocked about.

My aim in the following chapters is to illuminate the broad spectrum of abilities that you already possess. I will give you information and propose various exercises as well. Some of the exercises are simple, while some are more complex. You can do them all with confidence because they have been tested by countless participants in my storytelling workshops.

Beginning Your Training by Recalling and Observing Storytellers in Action

So as not to delay your training an instant longer, we are going to present you with the first four exercises. Don't put them off. Don't forget that what you learn depends on you. So, don't limit yourself to reading; do the exercises that are proposed.

Exercise 1. Try to remember a situation in which someone was telling you a story, a legend, an anecdote or a joke (these differences aren't important now). It doesn't matter whether you recall an incident from your childhood or from your recent past. Sit down in a comfortable chair, close your eyes, and try to reconstruct the situation with as many details as possible: where it happened; what the setting was like (its light, its colors, its smells); and who was telling it to you. What was the teller's voice like? What he was doing with his gestures and his eyes? Did he portray the characters? Did he imitate or parody their voices?

Exercise 2. Ask your siblings, parents, spouse, friends, fellow students or co-workers to tell you their stories of memorable experiences. You will be surprised at how varied the experiences are and how significant your informants find them. Most adults appear to have forgotten about them, and when you recall them together, both you and your informants will be surprised and excited. By asking careful and discrete questions, try to get each of them to reconstruct these experiences in detail. Your informants will be appreciative, and you will learn a great deal.

Exercise 3. Turn yourself into a "hunter" of spontaneous storytellers. Be attentive to whoever is relating some event either to you or to someone else. It doesn't matter what is being told or if the person has a special talent for it. Pay attention to everyone who relates something in everyday life. It makes no difference if the person telling is a child or an adult; observe him in the same way. Study him carefully: his connection to what he is telling, his attitude, his voice, his gestures—especially with his face, eyes and hands—his words, the rhythm of his movements, and the way he relates to his "audience."

Exercise 4. Carefully study a good teller on different occasions. Analyze his performance as we indicated in Exercise 3. Above all, observe how his behavior matches the story and the occasion, how he becomes involved in what he is telling, and how he varies his gestures and tone of voice.

After doing these exercises, you can decide whether or not to record your observations in writing. Depending on your personal style, you could find it useful to record them in a notebook. What is important is to do the exercises. You will learn to tell stories the same way good tellers do—through observing, listening attentively and, of course, practicing.

How to Tell Stories: A Latin American Perspective

CHAPTER TWO

WHAT TO TELL: FINDING AND SELECTING STORIES

What to tell? Since everything rests on a teller's desires, expectations and circumstances, the answer to this question will vary a great deal depending on who is telling the story and where and under what circumstances.

Selecting an appropriate story is necessarily based on the audience (age, occupation, personal interests, and cultural profile, for example), on the teller's personal interests, and on the specific circumstances in which the telling will take place.

Three General Criteria

■ *The Story's Appeal to the Teller*

So, what to tell? Both my own experience and that of many tellers whose activities I have studied lead me to conclude that, above all, storytellers must select a story that they themselves find appealing and interesting. They must feel the story and be drawn to it. If not, they will tell their story in a superficial, insincere, and empty way, without the interior resonance necessary to imprint the story with their own "charm."

■ *The Composition and Circumstances of the Audience*

Most of the tellers I have known don't usually limit themselves to one type of story. On the contrary, they tell different kinds of stories or tell the same story in different ways, depending on the circumstances. I remember, for example, the case of an excellent Guayúu teller who spent the afternoon in his arbor telling bawdy jokes for his friends and neighbors and then hours later, at nightfall, began to tell magnificent passages from myth for his family group. He gave great consideration and care to both types of telling. Reference is made in the preceding chapter to the practice in some villages of telling passages from myth in both a ritual and secular space-time framework.

From the point of view of the art of storytelling, therefore, there aren't any distinctions that would lead us to consider one kind of tale superior to another, be it a story, a legend, a family saga, a joke, an anecdote, a passage from myth or a historical episode. Such distinctions, which derive their relevance from social circumstances, are external to our art.

There are other factors, however, that play a role in determining the selection of a story. Not only must the story interest you, but it must also be capable of capturing your listeners' interest at the moment you begin to tell it. I remember a time when a group of friends and I were telling jokes while sailing in a dilapidated old boat on Lake Titicaca in Bolivia. Suddenly a storm came up. We continued telling jokes, perhaps in an effort to "put on a brave face." After a while, however, when we became terrified of capsizing, no one was laughing. In that solitary location and in those temperatures, of course, capsizing meant ending up at the bottom of the lake. That possibility brought to my mind some stories of spells from the lagoons of the Venezuelan Andes, and I began to tell them.

The group was immediately interested, and our guide told a story about some gold chains and other Incan treasures hidden at the bottom of the lake. With these tales, we kept ourselves entertained and distracted until the danger passed. I'm not suggesting here a blueprint for action; I'm merely offering a concrete example of how circumstances influence a group's interests.

■ *The Story's Appeal to the Listeners*

But there is more: the story must appeal to both you and your listeners to the extent that it can create an atmosphere in which you and your audience enter into a state of communion, or, in the words of Crisanto, a folk teller with whom I once discussed this subject, an atmosphere in which you and your listeners "experience a love affair." Crisanto captured with metaphorical clarity the unique relationship forged between a teller and his audience when everything goes well.

What is the significance of this criterion that the story must interest your audience? How are we to understand it? It isn't easy to answer these questions, and again it is a folk teller who gives us the key. Cheguaco once told me that what is imperative for audience enjoyment is that the audience "be convinced." For that to happen, not only must the teller have certain qualities, but the story must meet certain conditions in relation to the audience as well. In other words, the story must maintain an invisible relationship with the experience of those present.

From the point of view of the art of storytelling, for example, nothing in theory prevents telling bawdy stories to four-year-old children. The restrictions that prevent our doing so have their origin in prevailing moral standards. It would be senseless, however, to select that kind of story for an audience of four-year-olds because they couldn't understand and enjoy it, given their lack of relevant experience. The same would be true with children that age if, for example, we tried to tell stories about supersensory beings they have heard nothing of. Let's put our current confusion about a child's unlimited imagination aside. Anyone who has experience with children knows that their imagination is fairly limited because it necessarily works from information provided by their relatively limited experience. Because of their more limited experience, children can establish relationships more freely than an adult, who is usually more constrained by "logical thought," but nonetheless their experience and their imagination remain limited.

You will have to be concerned with selecting a story appropriate for your listeners; whether they are children or adults, you will need to take into account their potential to expand on the images, ideas, concepts and situations that you evoke. You must take into consideration, therefore, your audience's life experience. Don't understand this requirement in too exclusive or rigid a way, however. It is true that stipulations such as age, grade in school, daily life circumstances, and craft or profession are important. You should also bear in mind, however, that print, sound, and audiovisual media now make it possible for most urban, and even many rural, communities to integrate information from beyond their everyday lives and culture into their immediate experience. You should also remember that, in spite of prevalent prejudices, human beings have the ability to be moved in the face of beauty, even if the criteria for beauty differ from one culture to another. Hatred and love, happiness and sadness, pleasure and pain, fear and courage, day and night, sun and moon, rain and wind, all form part of the human experience even if we each "codify" them in our own way.

So, first choose an interesting story. Then decide if you would like to share it with your anticipated audience. Lastly, consider the story's likely attraction and appeal to your listeners. Elsewhere I have suggested that you not limit yourself to one type of story, such as tales. Being open to the great diversity of those narrative forms that easily lend themselves to your preparatory work—tales, anecdotes, jokes, legends, sagas, biographies, historical episodes, and life histories, for example—will have a positive effect on the development of your creative potential and, if it is of interest to you, community involvement.

Some Other Criteria

Just the same, we are going to introduce a restriction: the human being's limited ability to concentrate on a story. It is true that this limitation varies depending on the listeners involved, their age (a child's attention span is particularly limited), their customs, and the conditions of their immediate surroundings. There is one unfailing criterion, however: it is better to choose a short rather than a long story, especially if you are a beginning teller. Not even Homer told *The Iliad* or *The Odyssey* in one sitting. So, look for a relatively short story at first. A printed story should not be more than one or two pages of an average-sized book with average-sized type; an oral story should not be more three or four minutes long.

It is also a good idea to choose stories that have more action than description or subjective reflection. Of course, this criterion is not absolute. The choice will depend on the story in question, the audience, and your manner of telling it. It will also depend on your interest in applying the story to other ends. For example, if your purpose in telling the story is to encourage creative activity involving the plastic arts, then this criterion will be of little use.

It will also be easier at first to tell stories with a fairly straightforward line of action, with few digressions and adventures secondary to the plot. The same principle applies to the number of characters: the more there are, the more difficult it will be for you to tell the story well and for the audience to follow it. And even if you tell it well, your audience still won't remember it.

We also need to discuss certain kinds of stories that, in my opinion, aren't suitable to tell. While we recognize the significant potential for applying storytelling to education and to social development, we must remember that storytelling is an art, and we can't allow ourselves to undermine or pervert it. If storytelling is appreciated as an art, then the application of the story will be all the richer and more effective because it will be operating on individuals whose sensitivities have been heightened at that moment. That is why I find it counterproductive to use stories as "commercials" for children, who are the principal victims of this type of practice, such as "you must brush your teeth" or "you must obey your elders." It is true that stories express values and encourage behaviors, but please don't reduce them to that. You can achieve much more with stories: you can stimulate children's sensitivity, reflection and imagination; enhance their enjoyment of literature and the play of words; facilitate the development of their capacity for listening and for verbal expression; and, above all, affect their formation by giving them a more sensitive, playful, and expressive image of an adult. All this potential is more important that the "commercials" that they will ultimately reject, and rightly so.

I also think that if you are going to select your material with the aim of stimulating social development or cultural activity, you should be candid about it. The specific context of your storytelling application can present yet another factor in your selection of material. If your aim is to promote spontaneous storytelling among your listeners, for example, then you will want to take into account the fact that, as folk tellers are fond of saying, "one story draws out another." And this "drawing out" usually happens because of a similarity in subject (such as ghosts, floods, or travels), in character (Uncle Rabbit, Uncle Fox, or Juan Bobo, for instance) or in setting (distant villages, buses, mines, or markets, to name a few). Once when I was involved in telling fictional stories on a square in a blue-collar neighborhood in Caracas, it occurred to me, not without ulterior motives, to share a certain anecdote. Told to me by an old man from the same neighborhood, it was connected to the time when the area was first settled. The effect was immediate. Several local people started telling other anecdotes about the same period, and as a result some young members of a cultural group who were present were able to begin collecting the oral history of the neighborhood.

Where and How to Find Stories

Your next question will probably be, "Where am I going to get my stories?" You have more possibilities than you may realize. You can tell stories from collections of oral traditions, stories of oral tradition that you yourself collect, literary stories, and personal experiences or original stories.

The process of finding, selecting, and adapting a story is different for each of these categories. We will discuss the last of these processes, adapting a story, later in this chapter and in Chapter Three as well. But right now, let's turn our attention to the process of finding and selecting stories, focusing on the special features of each of these four categories.

1. Published Collections of Folktales

The collections of stories from different oral traditions are a wonderful source for any teller, and if you want to dedicate some effort to being a storyteller, you should begin making your own collection.

In principle, as far as the art of storytelling is concerned, there are no restrictions with regard to the origin of an oral tradition. So, from the perspective of our art, there is no reason why a teller cannot tell stories from anywhere in the world. In my opinion, the factors determining your selection of a given story continue to be the criteria stated above—your interest in the story and your desire to share it, its appropriateness for the audience, and the circumstances. Indeed, I believe that in these times of increasing dissemination of information, tellers could put print and audiovisual media to good use when building their repertoire.

Nonetheless, there are certain external factors that will probably lead you to prefer stories closer to your own cultural sphere. Without excluding from your repertoire folktales from cultures very different from yours, you can still favor stories from the oral traditions of your own ancestry or from the traditions that you assume have shaped the cultural identity of your listeners. Such a decision would be fully justified if your interest in the art of storytelling is prompted by a desire to participate in a given group's collective defining of its cultural identity. My decision to dedicate myself to storytelling directly derives from my interest in contributing to this process. I have always worked on the assumption, however, that the defining of a group's cultural identity should not be xenophobic and that my art should contribute to better understanding between peoples. As it happens, I have told stories in different countries and in different cultural traditions. We know that in every Latin American country, the cultural identity of its inhabitants is not characterized by uniformity but by extremely broad diversity. The population of any Latin American country is made up of the descendants of different indigenous and European ethnic groups. Most Latin American countries are inhabited by the descendants of different African ethnic groups, and in others the presence of Asian traditions is especially significant. The most salient feature of all Latin American countries is that of mixed races. What is one to do with this complex cultural identity? Ignore it? Or better yet, put it to use? In other words, look upon it not as an obstacle, but as a resource. Well, the decision is yours. It is strictly a personal one, external to our art.

When you come across a book of folktales, it is important to examine the relationship between the book and the oral tradition from which the stories come; you need to determine whether the tales have been recorded by a collector and transcribed "faithfully," whether they have been "adapted," or whether they are "free versions" where the author diverges from the given oral tradition that serves as the basis for the narrative. You can easily determine this relationship by reading the introduction to the book, and sometimes the jacket also provides this information.

Some books assert the authenticity of the collection. Generally speaking, these types of books are the most useful for a teller because he can develop his own versions of the collected texts. However, you can't completely trust the assertion that these texts are authentic. The Italians have a saying: "Traduttore, traditore" ("Translator, traitor"). This concern is true regardless of the translator's intentions, and it is most applicable to collectors of stories. Let's leave to one side the fact that many collections come into being in one language and then are translated into another; in this case, the unconscious "betrayal" is very great. With regard to a collection written in the original language, remember that collectors usually have the teller alone and separated from his audience so that he can recite his story into a tape recorder or, in not so distant times, dictate it bit by bit. This practice means that the story, which later will be "faithfully" transcribed, is in itself not "faithful" because it omits parts that the teller says when he is in front of an audience. But still more is missing: the story lacks what is impossible to collect, that is, what the teller typically says not with words but with his voice, his eyes, his face, his hands—his whole body—and even with his breath, his pauses, his rhythm and his silences. Books of folktales are like collections of embalmed butterflies or printed pictures of flowers. No matter how pretty the latter are, they have no fragrance, and their texture is nothing more than that of paper. You will have to add what these embalmed narrations lack through a process of adaptation. We must emphasize, however, that folktale collections are a wonderful and irreplaceable tool for any teller.

For the purpose of the art of storytelling, perhaps it would be better to consult a good adaptation of folktales made by a talented writer who is sensitive to oral tradition; since the vibrancy of those stories suffers when they are forcibly transmuted into writing, it is preferable that the writing at least attempt to return to them something of what they have lost. But in that case, how would you know how far the adapter's hand has reached? Here you will find it helpful to take into account both the "faithful" text and the adaptation. Still, given the prevalence of poor quality adaptations totally lacking in beauty even when made with good intentions, it is better to work with a "faithful" collection and make your own adaptations or free versions.

As for the third type of collection, the "free versions" based on oral traditions, you will have to treat them as literary stories, which will be discussed in the next section.

There is a fourth type of supposed stories of oral tradition. I am referring to the adaptations and versions made specifically for children. With few exceptions, they aren't a particularly suitable point of departure for preparing stories to be told live. Of little literary quality, many of them are basically nothing more than the pedagogical and moralizing designs of those who assume that "children's literature" is a pedagogical resource for "educating poor little creatures" supposedly incapable of making their own judgments and needing to be shielded from exposure to strong emotions. This type of adaptation results in boring and saccharine stories, and when faced with them, children often prefer the emotions that movies and television offer. What I have said here, of course, is not to be taken as a vote of approval for racism or as a defense of the violence and low aesthetic level of the majority of films and TV series for children.

Incidentally, several years ago the psychoanalyst Bruno Bettelheim touched off a significant controversy on the subject of fairy tales and "tales of magic" in general. Parents and teachers frequently ask me in my workshops whether these kinds of stories should be told to children. Two types of reservations are usually expressed. One type of reservation, doubt, or fear often relates to dramatic situations presented in the stories that were not originally intended for children. They were told and shared by young people and adults, and the presence of children was merely tolerated depending on the moral standards of the group and the time. Later, they became stories for children, and recently they have become "children's literature," undergoing various modifications in the process. Bettelheim has advocated through extensive and documented research that fairy tales are an invaluable source of aesthetic pleasure and moral and emotional support for children and that stories told by a parent offer children the opportunity to share their fears and anxieties. Now is not the time to consider these arguments in greater detail. I am undecided about the controversy, and besides, it is external to our art. I will simply say that the tales collected and disseminated by Perrault and the Brothers Grimm provide an excellent script for powerful tellings capable of capturing the attention of both children and adults. I enjoy these tales and sometimes tell them. If you are interested in becoming better acquainted with Bettelheim's arguments, you can consult his work listed in the bibliography.

There is another, though less frequent, type of reservation about these stories in Latin American countries. It is related to the fact that the tales are of European origin and "do not correspond to Latin American reality." It is quite true that the so-called "classical tales"—the stories of the Brothers Grimm or Perrault—are tales of European oral traditions that the Brothers Grimm and Perrault collected (we must refute once and for all the common misunderstanding that they "created" the stories). Given the predominance of European cultures all over the planet, these tales are usually accompanied by the adjective "classical," as are certain works of European music and literature. As for concern about the appropriateness of classical tales, I must repeat what I have already said: it is external to the art of storytelling. I find nothing wrong with including them in one's repertoire; it is a matter of personal choice. Although up to now I have primarily told Latin American stories, my own repertoire includes some classical tales as well.

In the kinds of collections discussed above, one finds not just "fairy tales" and "tales of magic" but also legends and myths, animal and comical tales, tales of terror, love, and adventure ... In short, in the world of collections, versions, and adaptations, there is something to suit every taste. I have put together a good personal collection of stories, and I am familiar with many more, thanks to libraries. There is little sense, however, in my recommending authors and editions that you probably can't find and at the same time omitting very good ones that you can. My recommendations will not be of titles of books, therefore, but of another sort. But first I will propose two new exercises; in this case you can delay doing them if you prefer.

Exercise 5. Go to the nearest library or, even better, to the city or national library. If you don't know how to look for a book in a library, don't worry. As a Venezuelan saying goes, "No one is born with experience." Don't be timid about turning to the librarian, who will most certainly be glad to help you. I have known many librarians, and most often they are people who love their work. In any event, I will give you some hints: the types of texts you need are usually classified under such titles as: "folktales," "native or indigenous stories," "folklore," "legends," "oral literature," "folk literature," "myths," "mythologies," "oral tradition," "popular traditions," and also under the name of the ethnic group, country or continent to which they belong.

Exercise 6. If you have the money, visit good bookstores and ask for collections or anthologies of "stories of oral tradition," "folktales," "legends", "native stories," or "myths." With at least one of these classifications you will surely make yourself understood even by the most uninformed bookseller.

2. *Collecting Folktales Yourself*

Collecting stories is not just the work of professional researchers. Storytellers do it in a more spontaneous and efficient way. Generally, the only record is the teller's memory or a simple note.

What to Tell

Collecting stories of oral tradition for your own telling is a beautiful, exciting and valuable undertaking. I don't hesitate to describe it this way. It is beautiful because it enables you to meet people and establish close, meaningful contact with them, and you may even encounter true storytellers if you work consistently and without haste. It is exciting because you feel that you are discovering hidden treasures. And it is valuable because you are helping to revitalize the given oral tradition you are in contact with. When you collect stories of oral tradition, you are helping to stem the loss of marvels in our modern, pressured lives, and you add one more step to the ongoing, daily defining of your audience's cultural identity as well as of your own.

How arduous you find your work to collect stories will depend on the social and cultural contexts you are dealing with, your creativity in taking advantage of them, and the degree to which the type of narrative material you can obtain coincides with your interests as a teller.

Above all, you must abandon the stereotypical idea that oral tradition stands on one side (with peasants and natives) and "modern" life on the other. Folktales among inhabitants of rural areas are interwoven with tales that are beyond their direct experience, thanks to the influence of print and audiovisual media. I have known peasant tellers whose repertoire included not only stories from their own oral tradition but also stories from other continents and even literary stories they had heard their grandchildren read from schoolbooks. I have also known folk tellers who learned stories from radio or television programs, cassettes that some traveler gave them, and movies they saw. I once encountered a folk teller vividly relating, as if it had happened on the Caribbean coasts, "The One-Eyed," his personal version of the film *Ulysses* based on Homer's epic; he had seen the film many years before in a movie theater in a nearby small town.

By the same token, it so happens that the presence of oral traditional tales is manifested in many ways in modern cities, and not just in print or in the mass media through soap operas, programs with audience participation, cartoons or films. Probably the closest that these tales can be found to you is in your own memory and that of your parents, your grandparents, or any relative or neighbor who is old enough. Immigrants, both foreigners and people from other regions of the same country, are usually careful to preserve some stories from their oral tradition, particularly if they come from rural areas. In all probability you can still find old stories among the inhabitants of the oldest neighborhoods in your city, among domestic servants (to whose hands and words many well-to-do families entrust the care of their children, who then grow up hearing peasant stories), and among barbers who have been at their work for decades. If you are a teacher, you can initiate a very valuable project and get some folktales into circulation if you ask your students to seek out stories among the oldest members of their families. You can also turn to the doorman or the cleaning staff of your school. You and the children will confirm the truth that not all knowledge is written or printed.

Let's try to do away with some other fairly well-established stereotypes. Oral tradition is not the trail of a comet that passed by thousands of years ago, leaving only its tail behind. It is a dynamic phenomenon that is continually developing new forms. A folktale doesn't live only in the memory of the elderly. In addition to being composed of more or less ancient elements (which, it must be emphasized, survive only if they are re-created), it is composed in the everyday creativity of people of all ages (and I have known excellent tellers of all ages) who transform anecdotes from everyday life into stories, who reshape old stories, and who create new jokes and new stories.

There are essentially two types of "traditional" tellers in modern cities. The type best known are mothers and grandmothers—and often fathers and grandfathers—who tell tales and stories to their children and grandchildren. But a second kind of teller is also quite prevalent, the one who tells anecdotes and jokes around the table after dinner, at parties and

What to Tell

bars, and in many other kinds of social gatherings. These tellers usually don't get the recognition they deserve because of their risqué tales, which people are in such a hurry to hold in moral contempt that they don't stop to appreciate the tellers' art, their stage performance, or their "gift." Of course, that doesn't prevent these same people from enjoying the stories. Sometimes the stories aren't vulgar but are truly humorous; nonetheless, the scourge of "seriousness" seems so widespread in our cities that those who don't laugh at them are seen as serious and responsible people. In the theater, this type of audience reveres tragedy and undervalues comedy. Oh, well, these are aspects of our harried, modern life—the miseries caused by various social pretenses. These serious people should listen to the wise words of José Julián Villafranca, a storyteller from eastern Venezuela, who once told me: "To tell stories is to have the art of a humorist. If a person lives all distressed, in a state of seriousness, he is prone to die suddenly and unexpectedly. Do you understand? Because it can cause him to collapse. Because his body has no fun; it's as if his body is in a prison without walls."

In short, if you start to remember the stories you have been told or if you listen attentively and sensitively to what you hear, if you adopt an observant and unprejudiced attitude, if you have a lot of patience and perhaps a small pocket recorder, or if you train your memory little by little and carry in your pocket a small notebook and a pencil, then you will be able to collect more—and better—stories than you think. Of course, you must never take your notebook out in front of a teller in the middle of his story; when he has finished, however, you can excuse yourself with some pretext such as going to the bathroom and then use your notebook to jot down what you would otherwise forget. On the other hand, you can use a recorder when your informant consents to it, even though you should avoid putting it right front of him. Remember nonetheless that unless you have some more systematic type of work in mind, it will always be better to let your informant tell his story in peace and reward him with your attention. If your only purpose is the teller's normal reason for looking for stories—that is, the desire to tell them—then it will be better if the storyline is entrusted to your ears and memory so that your eyes can observe your informant without the pressure of a recording device. Remember, as we have already noted, that the informant's gestures, looks, and manner will provide you with basic material for your later telling, and they won't be the same if there is a recorder in front of him.

If you proceed in this way, you will have plenty of material, and then you can choose what best suits your circumstances and interests. Continuing with the pattern we have established, we are going to suggest two exercises; as with the two previous ones, you don't have to do them right now. They can be postponed until you finish reading this chapter.

Exercise 7. Try again to remember one or more of the stories you heard. Do this calmly. Perhaps the story doesn't completely come back to you in one sitting. Do you remember some images from the story that particularly impressed you? What are they? What was happening in this story? You don't have to be exact. Try at least to give an approximate answer. Who were the characters? How did the story begin? How did it end? Have you succeeded in reconstructing it satisfactorily? If you haven't, it doesn't matter; maybe you will do it later today or tomorrow, when you are more relaxed and your mind is freer. Einstein used to say that his best ideas came to him when he was shaving, in other words, when he was more relaxed. Give yourself time. Meanwhile, go to the next exercise.

Exercise 8. Seek out a story or an anecdote. Don't take a recorder or a notebook; just take yourself and your enthusiasm. You don't know anyone who regularly tells stories, anecdotes or jokes? Well, he doesn't have to be an extraordinary teller. It's enough for this exercise that he be an ordinary teller. Think, think. What about your parents, your siblings, your spouse, your children, some distant relative, a neighbor, an old friend or your friend's parents? Have you thought of someone? Now go to this person, but proceed carefully, without inhibiting him. Find a suitable way to get him to start telling you a story. Have you found it? Now get ready to listen to him with interest. Let him tell you what he will, it doesn't matter; in principle, everything is of value. Rid yourself of prejudices; you can evaluate the quality of the material later. What is important right now is that you get him to tell you stories and that you manage to remember at least one of them. You will write it down when you have finished meeting with your informant or when you go home. Don't forget it; be alert the whole time, not to details but to what happens in the story, what it is about, who the characters are … You can postpone this exercise and continue reading but try to do it as soon as you can.

3. *Literary Stories*

Literary stories, that is, those created through the writing process, can be another interesting source for a teller. Usually a literary story is the work of the writer whose name appears on the publication.

We need to clarify that in spite of a generalized blending of literature and the art of storytelling, they are in fact two different disciplines. When I once told the renowned Venezuelan writer Oswaldo Trejo about my difficulties in telling most of his stories, his response was: "I write what I cannot tell; if I didn't write it, I would tell it."

The notion of "oral literature" has been spreading for a century. It began with the intention of certain European researchers, especially Paul Sebillot, to apply the notion of literature to "exotic" cultures and to certain European social groups who had not produced written works but among whom there were magnificent storytellers. Sebillot hoped that "oral literature" would "take the place" of literature in those groups. This hope was patently ridiculous since there was nothing to replace. At any rate, with the term "oral literature," Sebillot managed to replace a real phenomenon, the one that we have been calling the art of storytelling.

Certain "evolutionist" anthropological theories have claimed, without foundation, that the art of storytelling is the predecessor of literature. This claim has not been demonstrated, and nothing proves that stories that circulated orally served to inspire literary creators. If such a sequential relationship were true, then we tellers, much less those of us who fully participate in the social system of writing, would no longer exist, or else we would be something in the nature of pre-litterateurs and the art of telling would be pre-literature.

Now is not the appropriate time to expand on this subject. The interested reader can to turn to the studies that I have already dedicated to it and that are listed in the bibliography. For right now, suffice it to say that while written words are the only material that the writer uses to create his work, the teller uses words, voice, and body and facial expression, as well as his ability to portray characters, interact with the audience, and utilize space and objects. With these differences, it is obvious that the writer must make use of words in a completely different way since he can't rely on anything else to tell his story. It is important to understand that literary stories are very different from oral stories and are inevitably enjoyed by readers in a very different way from the way audiences enjoy stories that are told in their presence.

These differences between literary and oral stories have consequences for a teller's selection of literary stories to adapt and tell. Not all literary stories lend themselves to adaptation, and most of those that are "tellable" require careful reworking. The number of words in the story will most likely have to be reduced, and many descriptions, musings of the characters, and digressions from the main plot will no doubt need to be omitted. Be aware of these considerations, and don't prematurely reject a literary story just because of its length. You could also face the problem of not feeling comfortable with some of the ways the language is used. Since a teller doesn't memorize and recite the text, you will need to consider whether the story interests you enough to find suitable equivalents through different usage of language and through body movements or props; naturally, the equivalents would have to be in keeping with your style of telling.

When you are considering selecting a given literary story to adapt and tell, you will ask yourself, as usual, whether the story is interesting to you, whether you want to share it, and whether it is suitable for your audience. There is yet another issue to consider, beyond that of possible changes in the language: you must determine whether the crux of the story line has value in and of itself. If it does, you have a point of departure that justifies working on a good adaptation. This is an essential requirement, just as it is when a novel is brought to the movie screen or to the theater.

Ask yourself if the line of main action in the story is well defined. If the story is rich in digressions or if the protagonist's internal musings are essential, analyze how you could resolve these features when telling the story. Consider, moreover, whether the story is told in the first person or whether the narrator is a witness or is omniscient, capable of telling even what he didn't witness himself, such as the characters' feelings and reflections. Think about whether you would find these details manageable, how you would accomplish the changes, and what the consequences would be. I remember a workshop in Cordova, Argentina, when an attractive young woman told a story in the first person, saying at one point, "Then I took off my shirt, and with my bare chest …" For most of those present, the events recounted from that point on appeared quite incongruous because the male characters in the story seemed not to notice this nudity. We asked the young woman about it when she finished; the original story, she explained, was told by a male protagonist, and she had failed to make the necessary adaptation.

Don't be intimidated, however. My repertoire includes adaptations of many literary stories; I enjoy telling them, and they usually appeal to very different kinds of audiences. One particularly frequent question in my workshops has to do with the author's nationality. I think that the same considerations we discussed for stories of oral tradition are valid here. From the point of view of the art of storytelling, there are no restrictions with regard to the nationality of an author, just as there are no restrictions with regard to type of story. Everything is of value: horror stories and stories that are humorous, absurd, political, tragic, or erotic. Psychological and autobiographical stories can be more complicated, but there are no hard and fast rules, so don't hesitate to do your own exploring.

Finally, let me suggest that you consider adapting and narrating dramatic literature, a work written to be performed in the theater. This type of adaptation requires taking passages that are developed through dialogue and action in the original work and putting them into narrative form. It may be even more difficult if you decide to narrate poetry. I have included a few stories from these two literary genres in my repertoire, and I am pleased with the results. I suggest that you try them farther down the road.

Here are two new exercises for you:

Exercise 9. Go to the library and check out books of stories that you have previously read. Glance through the tables of contents and randomly skim over various isolated paragraphs in the stories. Try to remember and identify those stories that you liked or just the books that they were in. Set these books apart, keep them on hand for a few days, and reread those old stories in your free time.

Exercise 10. If you have the money, go to a good bookstore and ask about an anthology of short stories. Check it, see if it arouses your interest, and if so, buy it and start reading it.

4. *Personal and Original Stories*

Storytellers' personal experiences and stories of their own creation are a very important part of their repertoire. These stories can be in various

What to Tell

forms: jokes, anecdotes, sagas, tales, stories, *pourquoi* stories and legends. They can be true, fictional, or compositions of a mixed character. Folk tellers don't usually develop them in writing, but you may find it more comfortable to do so. If you write them out, keep in mind that you aren't dealing with a literary composition but with a story to be told to a live audience, so a handy, unencumbered note about what happened will be sufficient.

Anecdotes are the most common form of original composition in the repertoire of a folk teller. They usually originate from the teller's personal experiences and immediate surroundings, and occasionally they are learned and told by another teller. When I first began my activity as a professional teller, I was very focused on sharing "stories." The audience repeatedly told me, however, how much they liked the way I tied one story to another by telling an anecdote. I gradually discovered the power of an anecdote when it is appropriately selected and prepared. I also saw a connection between my natural tendency to tell anecdotes and that same tendency in numerous folk tellers, and conversations with them helped me to understand a little better the mechanisms that storytellers use for building their repertoire of anecdotes.

When I was taking drawing classes a few years ago, my teacher Abilio Padrón once came up to my drawing board and said: "Don't draw, observe." I immediately stepped back from my board and began to concentrate on the model in front of me. After a while I returned to the board to capture the result of this observation. Abilio again came up to me and gave me his judgment: "See, Daniel, I told you not to draw but to observe. Spend a long time observing patiently and actively. The artist must, above all, learn how to observe."

Storytellers and even their audiences have pointed out the same thing to me. I remember once talking with some customers in a bar in a small village in the Venezuelan state of Yaracuy. Referring to a renowned teller from the area by the name of Esteban, one of them told me, "There are people who avoid Esteban when a relative dies or when they are experiencing a painful situation because he observes and analyzes people when they cry and comes up with a story about it. He does the same thing with someone who laughs in a particular manner or has had too much to drink. Later he reinvents it. You see? It is his way of coming up with a story."

Similarly, storytellers and audiences from many different places have told me that the teller "takes his characters from daily life and gives them his own color, his own flavor." Once when I was in a cattle-raising area, a local resident spoke about his favorite storyteller. "He creates his stories by adapting misfortunes and adventures from daily work: an escaped bull, a pair of pants torn when the wearer bends down, any little thing." So, take heart because you can do the same thing! I usually ask workshop participants to tell an anecdote about something curious that has recently happened to them. Some begin by saying that nothing of interest ever happens to them. But after a while, stimulated by the stories of participants who are less constrained, they remember something, and a round of anecdotes is generated. It gains momentum on its own, and I often have to put an end to it so that we can go on to another exercise.

Exercise 11. Relax. Try to remember what you saw and heard in recent days on the bus, in the bank, in the bakery, on the street or at your job. Be thoughtful and recall the anecdotes that you heard so that you can add them to your collection. Think about the children you know and have contact with: they constitute an inexhaustible source of anecdotal moments. Being observant and attentive is what it is all about. Remember that anecdotes are not there waiting for someone to pass by and catch them like daydreaming butterflies. No, you must look for anecdotal facts and then adapt them, arrange them, work them as you please, like a "fibber" or, if this image helps you, like a gossipy old woman. Imagine what you can add and what you can take out with regard to the words, gestures, and character imitations, as well as the images and situations. And don't forget that it isn't a matter of a literary composition but of a story to be told. Perhaps in this moment a simple notation about what happened will suffice as a memory aid, or else a very short note in which you tell an absent friend what happened.

Surprise is important in a story, even a literary story, and that means that the story can't have either too many or too few elements. The Argentine writer Julio Cortázar once stated that a story must be as precise as the mechanism of a clock. This precision is even more important in the case of anecdotes: tellers always insist that they be short. For anecdotes as well as stories, many tellers also recommend creating intrigue and suspense and not giving the ending away at the start.

But you can also create stories, myths or legends in order to tell them. Perhaps this seems somewhat difficult for you now, but most likely you will change your mind as you continue to read this book and do the exercises. There are exercises in the next chapter for analyzing a story, and they will provide you with basic, useful, and versatile tools. For right now, however, let's turn to a simple example, that of *pourquoi* tales.

Pourquoi stories are a form of origin, or creation, myths. Creation myths are accepted as true in their own cultural setting, and all cultures have their own. They are stories of a sacred nature that explain the origin of man, of a people, or of the nature in which they live. In the contemporary western world, the most widespread creation myth is the Christian "Genesis" myth. In the last pages of this book, in the section of "Stories Ready to Tell," you will find fragments of grand mythological cycles that I have taken from various collections of folktales, commonly considered "oral literature."

A common trait of *pourquoi* stories is that they explain the origin of various beings and natural phenomena or their transformation to the aspect or appearance that they now possess. If you go to the final pages and analyze "The Firefly and the Blackberry Bush," for example, you will have a more complete understanding of the characteristics of *pourquoi* stories. I suggest that you read it before going on to the next paragraph.

One clearly sees in these stories that the origin or the transformation is explained in a "fantastic" manner, that is, in a way that has nothing to do with scientific studies of nature. This observation provides us with the key for creating *pourquoi* stories. We must first examine the world in which we live and assume that some being or natural phenomenon did not exist "when time began" or "when the world was being formed." Or, if it did already exist, then it did not look the way it does today. In the following exercises I propose some beginning lines of stories for you to expand on.

Exercise 12. Develop one of the following *pourquoi* stories:

- Long ago, when the world was being formed, butterflies were transparent. But it so happened that …
- Thousands and thousands of years ago, when the world began to take shape like the one we live in now, the sea did not have waves; rather, it was like an immense, calm lake. Then …
- In very distant times, when the sky was still being formed, there were no stars. Then …
- Long, long ago, when animals could still talk, giraffes did not have the long, elegant neck and legs of today. No, at that time they were short and …

As you can see, there are many possibilities for inventing stories. Just be very careful not to look for an answer that is too quick; give it the shape of a story, making it something that didn't happen instantly but rather has a history. One has to imagine a series of incidents that occurred until the phenomenon took its final shape. Don't forget a little suspense and remember also that you are dealing not with a literary composition but with a story to tell. Aim for simple language and, if possible, include some dialogue. Ah! Something else very important: don't forget that everything is possible in a story. So, don't let yourself be bound by a rational explanation; let your fantasy have free rein so that your ability to create an origin or transformation story can do its work.

Selecting Your First Two Stories

Well, if you haven't done them already, now is the time for you to do the exercises for finding stories that were suggested earlier (Exercises 5 and 12). Select at least two: an anecdote and a legend or a story. You can't delay doing the exercises any longer since the method used here is based on your learning through your own experience.

Exercise 13. Select an anecdote from your personal life.

Exercise 14. Select a story or a legend. It will be easier to start with one from oral tradition, but with the help of the exercises indicated above you could select a literary story. The story should be short, and you should have it in written form.

How to Tell Stories: A Latin American Perspective

CHAPTER THREE

PREPARING THE STORY TO TELL

People are often surprised at how many stories a professional teller knows, and they assume that storytellers have an extraordinary memory. They have a trained memory, to be sure, but something else—a "trick"—is at play. No teller memorizes a story word for word, and you won't either. Instead, you will just memorize its "structure," that is, the succession of actions or events in the story, along with the introduction and the ending. Nothing more.

Once you have chosen your story, you will first make a simple analysis of it. Then you will decide about some possible adaptations. Next you will work out the story's structure and decide whether you want to introduce any modifications to it. Lastly, you will learn the story. Thanks to the exercises you will do, all this will be an easier undertaking than you think.

I have chosen "Little Red Riding Hood," a commonly known story of European oral tradition, to exemplify the procedure and make it easier for you to follow the explanations. It is best to begin with the text of the story. I have turned to a publication that doesn't alter Perrault's original version of the folk tale, though I have modernized some of its archaic expressions.

Little Red Riding Hood *[Translator's Note 2]*

Once upon a time there lived in a certain village a little country girl, the prettiest creature ever seen. Her mother was very fond of her, and her grandmother doted on her still more. This good woman had made her a red cape with a hood, and it became the girl so well that everyone called her Little Red Riding Hood.

One day her mother, having just made some cakes, said to her, "Go, my dear, and see how your grandmamma is, for I hear she has been very ill. Take her a cake and this little pot of butter."

Little Red Riding Hood set out immediately to go to her grandmother, who lived in another village. As she was going through the woods, she met up with Gaffer Wolf, who had a very great mind to eat her up, but he dared not because some faggot makers were hard by in the forest. He asked her whither she was going. The poor child, who did not know it was dangerous to stay and talk with a wolf, told him:

"I am going to see my grandmamma and take her a cake and a little pot of butter from my mamma."

"Does she live far off?" asked the wolf.

"Oh, ay," answered Little Red Riding Hood; "just beyond that mill you see there, at the first house in the village."

"Well," said the wolf, "I will go and see her, too. I will go this way and you go that, and we shall see who will be there first."

The wolf began to run as fast as he could, taking the nearest way, and the little girl went by the longer path, amusing herself by gathering nuts, running after butterflies, and making bouquets of such little flowers as she found.

It was not long before the wolf reached the old woman's house. He knocked at the door—tap, tap.

"Who is there?"

"Your grandchild, Little Red Riding Hood," replied the wolf, imitating her voice. "I've brought you a cake and little pot of butter sent you by mamma."

The good grandmother, who was in bed because she was ill, cried out, "Lift the latch."

The wolf lifted the latch, and the door opened. Then he fell upon the good woman and ate her up in an instant, for it was above three days that he had not a bite to eat. He then shut the door and went into the grandmother's bed, expecting Little Red Riding Hood, who came some time afterward and knocked at the door—tap, tap.

"Who is there?"

Little Red Riding Hood, hearing the big voice of the wolf, was afraid at first, but believing her grandmother had a cold and was hoarse, she answered:

"'Tis your grandchild, Little Red Riding Hood, who has brought you a cake and a little pot of butter mamma sent you."

The wolf cried out to her, softening his voice as much as he could, "Lift the latch."

Little Red Riding Hood lifted the latch, and the door opened. The wolf, seeing her come in, hid himself under the bedclothes and said:

"Put the cake and the little pot of butter upon the stool, and come and lie down with me."

Little Red Riding Hood undressed and climbed into the bed. Once she was in the bed and noticed the very unusual shapes that her nude grandmother had, she was quite amazed.

"Grandmamma, what big arms you have!" she said to her.

"The better to hug you, my child."

"Grandmamma what big legs you have!"

"The better to run, my child."

"Grandmamma, what big ears you have!"

"The better to hear, my child."

"Grandmamma, what big eyes you have!"

"The better to see, my child."

"Grandmamma, what big teeth you have!"

"The better to eat you with, my child."

And saying these words, the wolf fell upon Little Red Riding Hood and ate her up.

Most likely you have missed the heroic appearance of the hunter who rescues Little Red Riding Hood and her grandmother from the bowels of the evil wolf. I regret that I must disappoint you: Little Red Riding Hood was never saved from the bowels of the wolf. At least, no heroic redeemer appeared in the original version published by Perrault. You will also have noted that in this version Little Red Riding Hood undresses and lies in the bed next to the wolf, believing him to be her grandmother. Only at that moment does she find her also nude grandmother strange and begin with her questions. And in spite of the bed and the nudity which might suggest a different ending, in this version the wolf still ends up eating her. Apparently, what have spread among us are different versions of the story, if not adaptations made for children. We must remember that like other folktales, this one was not meant specifically for children. Stories began to be transformed when the cultural environment changed, particularly when books became a part of civilization.

A brief analysis of "Little Red Riding Hood" will help us recognize the story's structural elements and make some decisions about adaptations.

Brief Analysis of the Story

A schematic questionnaire can help us. First, I will respond for "Little Red Riding Hood." Then I will propose the questionnaire as an exercise, and you will repeat it for the two stories you selected.

a. **Who are the characters?** The wolf and Little Red Riding Hood.
b. **Are there other characters? Who are they? What is their importance?** The mother and the grandmother. They are secondary.
c. **How do the events that are related begin?** With Little Red Riding Hood's departure.
d. **How do the events related conclude?** The wolf eats Little Red Riding Hood.
e. **What happened (in a few words)?** Little Red Riding Hood set off to her grandmother's to do an errand for her mother, and on the way, she encountered the wolf who asked her where she was going. Little Red Riding Hood gave him the information, and the wolf proposed that they race to her grandmother's house. The wolf arrived first, knocked at the door, pretended to be Little Red Riding Hood, and ate the grandmother. Then Little Red Riding Hood arrived, and the wolf ate her also.
f. **Is the sequence of the story linear? Or are there other supplementary events or digressions? What is their importance?** The sequence is linear. There are no other digressions.

g. **What is the position (explicit or tacit) of the narrator of the story?** *(Is he a participant in the events? Is he an eyewitness to the events? Were the events told to him by another person? Is he an omniscient observer of the events? A kind of "God" who knows what the characters feel and think?)* He is an omniscient observer. He knows, for example, that the wolf wanted to eat Little Red Riding Hood when they met in the forest and even knows why he didn't do it.
h. **Where do the events take place?** In a village in a forested area, without further specifications.
i. **When did the events take place?** In an indefinite time.
j. **Are the vocabulary and the use of the language common to yours?** In general, yes, except for a couple of words (gaffer and faggots).

The first four questions of the questionnaire (a-d) help us to identify the information necessary to outline the story's structure, as we did in our extremely brief response to the fifth question (e). The remaining questions help us to make some decisions about adaptation.

Adapting the Story

Since we are dealing with a folktale, which has a linear structure, no special adaptations are necessary in order to tell it. Perhaps the situation would be different with a literary story.

Moreover, the combination of the answers to questions g, h, and i lead me to accept without any problem keeping the same type of narrator. The decision would be different however, if, we were dealing with the story of a character who, for example, had witnessed events that happened two centuries ago or in another galaxy.

The vocabulary doesn't place great demands for adaptation, except perhaps for the words "gaffer" and "faggot." The first thing to do, of course, is look them up in a dictionary. We learn that a "gaffer" is "an old man, especially one from the country" and that this word is used either contemptuously or humorously. "Faggots" are "sticks, twigs, or branches" used primarily for fuel. These are not words that I use, and they don't play any special function in the story that I want to keep. I decide, therefore, to substitute "woodcutters" for "faggot makers" and to dispense with the word "gaffer." Since the story loses nothing if Little Red Riding Hood is carrying only a cake, I decide to do away with the butter. Of course, she could also carry a pot of butter, but in this case, I have decided that she will carry only cake. Moreover, to reclaim an image that my mother used when she told me the story and that is therefore a cherished image deeply engraved in my memory, I decide that Little Red Riding Hood will carry "a little basket with pastries." This decision doesn't have any effect on the essence of the story, and recapturing an image that is close to me will favorably affect the quality of my later telling.

There are other minor lexical adaptations needed for the story to be more understandable to contemporary listeners. I will put the woodcutters "nearby" instead of "hard by" in the forest; the wolf will say "Where are you going?" rather than "Whither are you going?"; and I'll say that the wolf hadn't eaten for "over three days" instead of "above three days." There aren't any other lexical adaptations to make in this story, but there are other changes that I, as the future teller, simply want to make. Again, it is a matter of minor adaptations that don't affect the story substantially but allow me to make changes I find appropriate. We will comment later on the greater or lesser relevance and legitimacy of these changes. In the meantime, let us continue with our adaptation.

In order to reclaim another image from the story as my mother told it to me, I have opted for making the grandmother live in the forest. I like it better that way, and, besides, I find it more convincing. If the grandmother lives in a village, it is more difficult to believe that the wolf can commit all those misdeeds without being found out by a neighbor. I also decide that it is more believable if opening the door requires taking a key from under the mat; since there are dangerous wolves about who are capable of lifting latches, it is harder to accept that the door would not have been locked with a key. For similar reasons I decide that when the wolf lies down in the bed, he puts on the grandmother's nightcap: the nightcap makes it more credible that Little Red Riding Hood doesn't notice the wolf's presence as soon as she opens the door. Besides, I think that it makes for an amusing image.

However, I think that Little Red Riding Hood would be too suspicious to get into the bed since she would be aware of the difference between the size of the wolf and that of her grandmother, even under the sheets. Therefore, I won't have her undress or lie down, or even leave the cake or the pastries on the stool; instead, I will have her interrogate the presumed grandmother right after she enters the house. Another reason for this modification is that I had initially chosen this story for a group of young children, and I prefer not to put an image of imminent animal-rape before them. This adaptation is of a different kind from those discussed above. This is no longer a matter of a simple detail; it is a major change. Nonetheless, I feel justified in making it. Otherwise, I wouldn't tell the story to children but would rather save it for adults. Perhaps I would develop two versions. We will return to the legitimacy of these kinds of changes later.

Let's turn now to establishing the structure of the story.

Structure of the Story

How do you prepare the "structure" of the story? It is very easy. You simply answer the question "What happened?" without omitting anything important in the development of the story. We find our point of departure in the answers to the schematic questionnaire presented earlier. But for the questionnaire, the answers were deliberately simple. Now we have to take into account some of the actions that we left out. This time we are interested in the succession of essential actions between the beginning and the end of the story.

Let's return to Little Red Riding Hood to illustrate the procedure. We take a sheet of paper and divide it lengthwise into two equal columns. In the column on the left we will note down, one by one, the "Principal Actions" that actually happened, that is, strictly speaking, the "structure." In the column on the right we write down the "Dialogues and/or Complementary Details" that correspond to each principal action; we will focus our attention on these elements of the story whether they are in their original form or are the result of modifications we made. The "Introduction," that is, how we anticipate beginning our story, and the "Ending," what we plan to say to finish the story, will be written separately. Let's see how everything looks in outline form.

"Little Red Riding Hood"

Introduction: Once there was a little girl who lived with her mother, and whose grandmother lived in the forest. Because the girl always wore a red cape with a hood, she was called Little Red Riding Hood.

Principal Actions	Dialogues and/or Complementary Details
1. Little Red Riding Hood's mother sent her to her grandmother's house.	1. The grandmother was sick, and Little Red Riding Hood's mother sent her daughter to take a basket of pastries to the grandmother.
2. Little Red Riding Hood took the forest road.	2. Little Red Riding Hood was carrying a basket with the pastries, which smelled delicious.

Principal Actions	**Dialogues and/or Complementary Details**
3. As she was walking through the forest, the wolf appeared.	3. He had been following her for a while, hiding among the trees.
4. The wolf wanted to eat her but at that moment didn't dare to do so.	4. He didn't dare to because there were some woodcutters nearby.
5. The wolf asked Little Red Riding Hood where she was going.	5. Putting on his most innocent face.
6. Little Red Riding Hood told him that she was going to her grandmother's house behind the mill.	6. Little Red Riding Hood didn't know that it was dangerous to stop and talk to the wolf.
7. The wolf proposed a challenge: each of them would go to the grandmother's house by a different path.	7. When proposing the challenge, the wolf spoke in a nonchalant way, as though the matter were not of particular interest to him.
8. Little Red Riding Hood accepted and continued along the main road.	8. The girl walked slowly and entertained herself by picking flowers and nuts and chasing butterflies.
9. The wolf took a short cut and arrived at the grandmother's house first.	9. The wolf ran.
10. The wolf knocked at the door, pretending to be Little Red Riding Hood.	10. "Knock-knock." "Who is it?" "It's your granddaughter, Little Red Riding Hood, come to bring you some pastries that my mother has sent you."
11. The grandmother had the wolf come in.	11. He looks for the key under the mat and opens the door.
12. The wolf ate the grandmother up.	12. He ate her in one gulp because he hadn't eaten in three days.
13. The wolf put on the grandmother's nightcap and crawled under the sheets.	
14. Little Red Riding Hood arrived at the grandmother's house and knocked at the door.	14. "Knock-knock." "Who is it?" "It's your granddaughter, Little Red Riding Hood, come to bring you some pastries that my mother has sent you."

Preparing the Story to Tell

Principal Actions	Dialogues and/or Complementary Details
15. The wolf, mimicking the grandmother's voice, had her come in.	15. She looks for the key under the mat and opens the door."
16. Little Red Riding Hood entered.	
17. Little Red Riding Hood found her grandmother's appearance strange and began to ask her about it.	17. "Grandmother, what big eyes you have." "The better to see you with." "Grandmother, what big ears you have." "The better to hear you with." "Grandmother, what a big mouth you have." "The better to eat you with!"

Ending: And the wolf swallowed her up in one gulp.

The "structure" of the story, then, is that succession of actions that we have called "principal" and have put in the left column. To establish what they are, you simply answer the question "and then what happened?" and nothing else.

It is easy to verify whether the structure has been set up correctly. If it has, then when you read the introduction—the left column—and the ending, you should have a coherent and continuous story, without needing to look for information in the column on the right except for the connection with the ending. In addition, if it has been set up well, it won't have any unnecessary details. After establishing the structure, you should do two vertical readings, the first to verify that nothing is lacking and the second to assure that nothing is superfluous; any necessary corrections are then made. As for the column of "Dialogues and/or Complementary Details," you should note down only those details and dialogues, or even metaphors and poetic images, which you want to retain from the original or from the adaptations that you decided on; of course, you may wish to introduce details that enrich the story. But it wouldn't be effective to include in the right column everything that wasn't included in the left. You have to be selective.

If you carefully analyze the column on the right in our example, you will see new adaptations and even additions. For example, the dialogue at the end seemed more interesting to me if the wolf used the pronoun "you," referring to Little Red Riding Hood, in each of his responses to her so that all of them would be consistent with the ending "the better to eat you with." That is my personal decision. Another teller could decide something different, and in principle it would be only different, neither better nor worse. You can also see the addition of details like the wolf "had been following her for a while, hiding among the trees" and "putting on his most innocent face," images that appeal to me as a part of the story I anticipate telling, especially with regard to gestures and body expression. (Little by little you will learn to anticipate how you will tell your story when you are making decisions about adaptations). These images came to mind as I was preparing the outline, and since I didn't want to forget them, I wrote them down.

Importance of the Structure of the Story

You can establish the structure as we have done here not only in tales but in any other type of narration: anecdotes, jokes, stories or legends. As the word suggests, the structure is the framework of the story, its skeleton. It is the basis of everything else. If you correctly establish and learn it, you have the key to achieving clarity in your telling, and it is extremely important that your story be clear.

The audience, professional tellers, and folk tellers all find clarity in the structure of the story to be crucial. Once an extraordinary Andean teller named Mano Chico told me:

You have to be intelligent to tell stories. You have to be intelligent if they are to turn out well and not be "bungled." A story has to be well prepared if you're going to tell it right and not bungle it by having what ought to come first come later, and what ought to come later come first. No, that doesn't work and people lose interest; the story has its own pattern, its own arrangement.

I have known several scarcely literate folk tellers who carry a little notebook where they write down a sort of summarized structure of each story, even of the shortest jokes: "I had a little notebook, which got lost, where I had written down this or that story, how it started or what it was called, and more or less what happened," José Isabel, a great teller of anecdotes and ancient stories, once told me. Another advantage of preparing a written outline (structure and complementary details) of each story is that this practice enables you to accumulate a growing repertoire and, with time, you can easily select what to tell when you want to prepare a storytelling session. I always prepare my stories this way. I have been able to build an archive of outlines; it contains stories that I once prepared for a special occasion and haven't told again for years, but if and when I want to use them again, I already have a solid point of departure.

Your First Two Stories: Analysis, Adaptation, and Preparation of the Outline

You have seen how to do it. Now it is your turn. Are you ready? Take the time to analyze the two stories that you selected earlier. If for some reason you later decide to use two other stories, this is still the procedure you will follow.

Exercise 15. Read and reread—thoroughly and analytically—both of the stories you selected. Now answer, first for the anecdote and then for the story or legend, the same questions that we formulated and answered for "Little Red Riding Hood." (You can choose between answering verbally or in writing, but in any case, your answers should be precise).

Exercise 16. Work out the outline (structure and dialogues/complementary details) of the anecdote you selected.

Exercise 17. Work out the outline (structure and dialogues/complementary details) of the story or legend you selected.

In preparing the outline, you can take into account the preceding example of "Little Red Riding Hood" as well as any of those found at the end of this book in Part III: Stories Ready to Tell. Don't forget to check the column on the left to be sure that you haven't either left anything out or added something unnecessary. You will find Exercises 16 and 17 easier to do if you postpone most of your adaptation decisions for the five exercises below since they are specifically designed for the adaptation process.

Have you done both of the above exercises? If not, there isn't any sense in going on because you won't have the groundwork for it. The method proposed here is not based on your simply reading the book and doing everything in your imagination but rather on your doing the exercises one by one as you read the book. If you don't comply with this strategy, it will be far more difficult for you to develop the skills and dexterity that the book proposes to encourage and that you will need to achieve your final goal of a successful storytelling experience.

Exercise 18. Reread the column on the left for your anecdote. Analyze it carefully and make sure that you are not giving away the ending ahead of time. This is a mistake that people often make in everyday life when they tell an anecdote. Now reread first one column and then the other and think about whether you are pleased with the outline. Or could it be arranged, or "ordered," as tellers say, so that the story would be more interesting and amusing? If so, you can take things out or put them in; you can change whatever you want—characters, circumstances, or context. The anecdote is entirely yours, and you can do what you want to with it.

Exercise 19. Reread the column on the left for your story or legend. Decide whether you are satisfied with the development of events as presented or whether you would prefer to introduce some changes. Don't dismiss that possibility ahead of time.

Exercise 20. If you prefer a different development, examine the type of material that you have selected to tell:

If this were a matter of a literary story and you were proposing to make a recording of it instead of telling it live, you would contact the author so that he not only would authorize you to record it but would also accept your adaptation. But this is not the case. Your concern is strictly a question of personal ethics and of evaluating whether the decision is feasible in view of the ends you hope to achieve. If you wanted to acquaint a literature class with a story by a given author, it would be to your advantage to make the necessary adaptation to enable you to go from a written work to live art; nevertheless, you can't alter the course of the story because such a modification could confuse your students. If you aren't going to use the story for a class, however, you can certainly introduce changes that seem fitting to you. A compromise solution is always appropriate: you can inform your audience about the kind of changes you have introduced after—but never before—telling the story.

If you are working with a story from oral tradition, what importance does that tradition have for you and for your audience? What is the significance of your faithful adherence to the structure of the story? The story isn't anonymous. While it doesn't have an author with a first and last name, it is, in effect, a collective creation, and it is historically valued by some culture on this planet. It doesn't matter which one; the exquisite creation of any people merits your respect. It would probably show poor judgment on your part to change the structure of the story. Precisely because you value the story highly, however, you may feel drawn to modify it and thus give it new life. The oral tradition is not immutable, as widespread prejudice would have it; on the contrary, it is flexible, with great capacity for change and adaptation. Whether consciously or not, even "traditional" tellers change stories with time. There are studies about this phenomenon, and the reasons for it have even been explained: forgetfulness, adaptation and omission of strange circumstances, modernization, fusing stories, incorporating elements from other stories, and adapting the setting, among others. As you see, reasons abound for justifying adaptations that you will consciously make. Besides, if you find it necessary and appropriate, you can always inform your audience about the changes you have made after you have told your story.

Exercise 21. In addition to substantial changes in the structure, examine the possibility of other, minor adaptations that would be reflected in the column on the right. In particular, take into account that in the right column you didn't write down everything that wasn't a principal action but only what you found important to preserve from the original text. Adaptation is not only taking something out, it is also changing something as well as introducing something new. If you are dealing with a folktale, bear in mind that it lost much of its life, its "flesh and blood," when it was reduced to a written transcription. Likewise, with regard to a literary story, don't forget that your work will involve a very important change in language; you will use images and words in a different way from the author of the written text. In any event, don't proceed in a cold and technical manner. Give your imagination a chance to play. Reread the story and try to re-create it in an imaginative way; when you encounter problems, seek solutions to them with care. Don't rush yourself, give yourself time; this activity can be very gratifying.

Exercise 22. Pay special attention to possibly converting narrated passages into dialogue. If you use your imagination, your story will definitely be enhanced. Try to imagine the characters that participate in the dialogues; they should each have their own way of speaking. This is a very important exercise, and if you do it right, you will tell your story in a more dynamic and appealing way.

How to Tell Stories: A Latin American Perspective

CHAPTER FOUR

PREPARING YOURSELF TO TELL THE STORY

Like many peasant and indigenous tellers, I have known in Latin America, Japanese tellers maintain that there are no good or bad stories, only good or bad tellers. A bad teller, they say, can ruin the best story, just as a good teller can delight his audience even when telling a dreadfully bad one. It is crucial, therefore, that you be prepared to tell your story.

I have known storytellers of the most varied styles imaginable, but the good ones always have something in common: they succeed in making their listeners believe, and even more, imagine and feel, what they are telling. They themselves imagine and feel it. They fully believe in what they are telling, at least while they are telling it. If you think back on your observation exercises, you will come to a similar conclusion.

Use your memory; that is your point of departure. Try to picture one of your recent observations of a story being told; evaluate the importance of the teller's conviction that what he was relating was true even if he was a casual teller recalling a personal experience. Assess the degree to which his conviction added strength, value, and meaning to what he was saying.

The audiences of famous tellers appreciate this point. A frequent attendee of performances by the extraordinary teller Franciscote once commented: "There are many people who tell stories, but few who do it like Franciscote. You have to understand that he tells a story as if he believed it, even though he knows it isn't true." The German teller Erika Schwab, who some decades ago lived in a Venezuelan village where she told stories in the public library, said to me: "I feel what I tell; if I tell you, for example, about a person who runs and runs and runs, I feel myself running. I feel what each character is feeling, I concentrate, I forget everything else, and I am in the story. I feel the story, and I think that if I feel the story, everyone else can feel it." It is precisely this belief in the story, shared by the teller and the listener, that assures the success of a telling. If the telling is good, then both the audience and the teller will find their imagination and emotions richly stimulated. Luis Luksic, a magnificent veteran teller, was convinced of this connection between a good telling and the stimulation of the imagination. As he once explained to me: "I always give pieces of colored chalk to children when I tell because it's absurd for the teller to think that he is the main star. No, the main star is the audience. And when I finish telling a story to children, I have them draw pictures so that they can capture what they've been imagining throughout the telling."

Experience indicates that only when the teller feels and imagines what he is telling does his audience feel and imagine it, too. But the teller and the audience don't feel and imagine exactly the same thing—not at all. What the teller and each member of the audience feel and imagine is related to what we will call each person's "personal archive." The storyteller projects open images that carry many meanings, and the listener processes them and re-creates them in his own way, from his own experience.

What is the source of the material which tellers draw on to re-create a story and which enables the listener to re-create the images they project? Both teller and listener work with their "personal archives" of images and emotions. To one degree or another, these images and emotions are long-standing and are both conscious and unconscious; they have been experienced, heard about, read about, or seen in photographs or films. To one degree or another, they have been transformed or modified with regard to the real events that gave rise to them and are now associated and fused with each other. They all come from the personal experience of the individual in question. The process of telling activates these archived images and emotions, and as they are evoked, associated, disassociated, and transformed, new images and emotions are created. Like the actor and his audience, the teller realizes an act of evocation and re-creation through the work of his imagination. The audience is rarely conscious of this. The teller, like the actor, is aware of it. A good part of an actor's or professional teller's self-preparation specifically involves both the development of his re-creative capacity through the evocation of imaginary material and the enrichment of his personal archives through experience and observation.

The Venezuelan folk teller José Jiménez explained what makes an audience laugh as follows: "The people are imagining what's being told to them, and they laugh because the story reminds them of the mischief and tomfoolery that they've experienced themselves, and that's why they laugh." This phenomenon is not limited to mischievous stories, however; laughter occurs with every type of story.

Franciscote, the peasant teller from whom I have learned so much, explains the teller's re-creative evocation like this: "When I begin telling the story, then the sense of it becomes clearer to me, and the words come to me more easily. Because your memory comes into play when you are telling, and the sense of the story becomes clearer to you." Bertha Vargas, another excellent teller, once expressed it like this: "At those moments I have my head full of … I don't know how to explain it … what I am telling." José Moreno, an Andean teller, maintained: "It's the same as if it were happening to me, I seem to be seeing all of it."

Re-Creative Evocation, Imagination, Memorization and Telling

Let's see then what you can do to learn the story so as to tell it vividly. Above all, you must reflect on your own previous experience with telling and realize that you, too, possess the capacity for re-creative evocation and that you routinely use it in order to relate any personal experience you want to share with others. Try to reconstruct a time when you told how a traffic accident occurred, or something curious happened, or a child misbehaved. You will see that as you recounted the event, images and emotions that you originally experienced came back to you, not necessarily in a connected way, and it was specifically on the basis of these emotions and images that you wove your tale. What makes this phenomenon possible is the deep impression the event made on your senses and the effect it had on your feelings.

What you must do now is successfully train that capacity and apply it to telling all types of stories, whether true or fictional. Let's do a series of exercises with that goal in mind. The first two are preparatory in nature; the rest focus on the stories you selected. These are stimulating exercises even if they seem a little strange to you. You can accept them without constraint; they have already been done by thousands of people, and without exception they have proven useful and enjoyable.

Exercise 23. Choose a place such as your bedroom that is relatively quiet and dark. Make sure you are comfortably dressed. Take off your shoes and lie on your back on your bed or on the floor. Stretch out your arms and legs comfortably. Open your hands and relax them. Relax your whole body. Close your eyes gently, without pressing your eyelids, and breathe deeply, calmly, and slowly until you feel completely relaxed. Then remember any moment of great happiness in your life. It doesn't matter which one, the first one that comes to mind. Yes, it will be best if you select just that one, the first one that comes to you. What was happening at that moment? Where did it happen? Who was with you? What was the place like? What objects were there? How did the light play on them? Where was the light coming from? What were the colors and the sounds of the moment? And the smells and the tastes? What was the texture of the things that you were seeing and feeling? Use all five senses—sight, hearing, taste, smell, and touch—to slowly reconstruct the images of that occasion. Do it little by little; there is no rush.

Exercise 24. Try to do this exercise in a place similar to the one in Exercise 23. Stretch out calmly, breathe, and relax just as you did before. Put on some music, preferably a record or cassette, but possibly the radio, too. If the latter, try to choose some program or station that doesn't have frequent commercials. If you can select the music, choose whatever you prefer; it doesn't matter whether it is vocal or instrumental. In any event, you will be relaxed with your eyes gently closed, and you will completely give yourself over to the sounds. It is very important that you concentrate all your attention on them. Don't linger on any idea or thought; resist doing so, and let them pass by like clouds pushed by the wind. Take pleasure in the situation for as long as you want and then play at imagining something, it doesn't matter what, that the music suggests to you. Again, it doesn't matter what. Give yourself over to those images.

These two exercises will allow you to discover—if you haven't done so already—your capacity for playing imaginatively with sensory images and feelings and for giving yourself over to them. This imaginative play is what good tellers engage in when they tell, though in a controlled fashion since they are necessarily constrained by the story and the circumstances in which it is told, and herein lies a good measure of their success. If you want to improve each time you tell, therefore, you have to train this capacity. I recommend that you repeat these exercises now and then. The first time you do them, you will make some discovery, and you will become sensitized. As you continue to do them, you will make new discoveries; you will enjoy them more, and little by little you will learn how to control the process. Optimizing your personal powers in this way will enrich your qualities as a human being.

Now I am going to propose some exercises for applying this same procedure to the stories you selected.

Exercise 25. Sit down comfortably someplace where it is quiet and where you won't be interrupted; now slowly read one of the stories you selected. Give yourself time to let what is happening in the story touch you as much as if you were witnessing or participating in the events. If there is a flower in the story, become aware of its fragrance, see its colors, feel the roughness or the smoothness of its stalk, the softness of its petals … . Re-create each image of the story in this manner. Give yourself the chance to enjoy the reading.

When you have finished this exercise, go immediately to the next one.

Exercise 26. Stay seated comfortably in the same place. Let your arms fall to your sides, stretch out your legs, and let your chin fall on your chest. Concentrate your attention on the story that you have just read and enter into it, into its world, though in a way unnoticed by the characters, as if you were a kind of "God" observing everything from above and capable of feeling what each character feels. You can see everything from your high place, you can feel the floor with your feet, and you can experience your own actions and those of the other characters. Then focus on any moment of the story and begin to "become" each character, to embody him or her, to feel, hear, and see as if you were that character. Carefully reconstruct each detail that might be important. If there are animal characters, don't forget the importance that smells and movements have for many animals. Take delight in seeing each scene as in a movie and in entering into and moving out of the film at whim. Then, go to another scene of the story; go to any scene, to the one that comes to you without your thinking about it or stopping to select it. Continue the exercise until you are tired or until it gets late because you certainly won't be bored.

Once you have done these two exercises with one of the stories, you have two choices: you can do these same exercises with the other story and then pass on to the next series of exercises, or you can do the next series first and after finishing them, do all the exercises with the other story. In any event, once you have completed the above exercises, you deserve a rest because you have worked much harder than you realize. You have made a powerful imaginative effort, and it is good for you to be distracted for a while. Only then can you do the exercises that follow.

Exercise 27. Find the outline for one of the two stories you prepared with the exercises from the preceding chapter; the story you just used for doing Exercises 25 and 26 is preferable. Read silently—or aloud, if you prefer—the left column of the outline a few times, re-creating it with the help of the right column and your memory of the emotions and sensations. Then, memorize the introduction, the left column, and the ending until you can repeat them aloud without hesitating. You will see that it's easy for you to do this now.

After finishing this exercise, go to the one below.

Exercise 28. Sit down or lean back comfortably and one by one review the images from the introduction, the succession of events, and the ending; try to re-create them in your imagination in great detail, entering into each character as before.

When you have done this exercise, go immediately to the next one.

Exercise 29. Either seated or standing, tell the story to a chair, a broom or your cat—it doesn't matter. You will be the first to be surprised at the results. After you do the same thing again, you will feel confident and articulate, and then you will almost be ready to tell the story to your children, friends or students. I hope it is clear that you won't memorize the words; instead, you will call to mind the sequence of main actions (the sequence that you organized in the left column of the outline) and improvise your words.

Exercise 30. It will be fun for you to tell the story again to a broom, a vase, or the cat, without saying anything out loud. You will have to tell it exclusively through movement and gesture. It won't be your aim to depict each segment of the story through mime but rather to make your spectator-object feel the story. After a while, however, you will see that you are indeed engaged in mime, and other body movements and gestures will come to you.

This exercise may seem unreasonable at first, but it is very useful. On the one hand, it will allow you to discover possible gestures for the story in question, some of which you will use when you tell to an audience. On the other hand, it will improve your dexterity in expressing yourself with your body. I have suggested it for workshop participants on many occasions, and even extremely timid people have participated, finding it fun and interesting once they overcame their initial stage fright. Don't fail to do it!

The next exercise will prepare you to appreciate the value of vocal nuances, narrative rhythm, and silences.

Exercise 31. Make a tape recording of your story and then listen to it. Draw your own conclusions and then retell it, introducing changes that seem appropriate to you. Once you are at this point, you are certainly in a position to give a very good retelling of your story. Nonetheless, I am going to propose a final series of exercises that will make your telling even more appealing to your audience and particularly delightful for you. When I spoke earlier of adapting a story, I suggested that if it lacked spoken conversation, you might try transforming some narrative passages into dialogue. The best tellers regularly turn to this resource to engage their audience, and they use it in a very special way, employing a form of mimicry when they imitate or portray the conversing characters' speech and actions. You can do this, too. Your success will depend on your sincere dedication to "living" these roles and on your work to experiment with them.

Observation, the Work of the Imagination, and Character Portrayal

Storytelling audiences always consider the portrayal of characters to be very important. An admirer of Don Inocencio, an old peasant teller, once said to me: "The people enjoy him because he depicts the actions of the characters; he gets in a firing position, he makes the noise of the shot and even of the falling animal. He has a lot of imagination. It's as if he were all of them." Tellers also agree on this point. Cheguaco, an extraordinary teller from Margarita Island, for example, told me about his admiration for the style of his predecessor Gil Chaleco: "He was a theatrical teller because if he needed to move from one place to another, he moved; if he needed to use a lot of mimicry, he used it. It was all about his being able to get through to the group of listeners and make them think only about what he was telling; he lived the characters through his words and gestures." Or, as Jorge Cabello, another great teller, explained it: "Mimicry and characters are what gives the story its charm because the people not only listen but also see and laugh more; it is like comparing radio and television."

Oliva Torres, one of the best tellers I have ever known, offers us an important key to character portrayal. Let's listen to what was occurring as she portrayed an elderly woman: "It's as if I were the old woman I'm telling about and the image of my father telling to me, because he had immense charm and appeal; he was wonderful at making people laugh and at using his body. I'm totally focused, as if I were seeing the old woman, and since she smells like an old person, I sense that smell, the image and the form of being the old woman, her eyes, and her mouth, and I imagine to myself that she is wearing an apron, dressed like the witch La Voladora [a character from another of her stories]." Oliva continued her explanation with her body, imitating the old woman.

This revelation of one of Oliva's trade secrets is very valuable. Note that she did something that you have already practiced. She was carrying out a work of the imagination, evoking material from her personal archive and re-creating it so as to see and feel the old woman. This activity is very similar to what you learned to do in order to tell your story, but Oliva applied it to a character. She channeled the re-creation toward an imitation, toward giving her body over to the character without inhibition or embarrassment.

There are two types of situations: you know the character of the story (in the case of anecdotes that come from your personal experiences) or you don't (the character comes from fiction or from a story told to you by someone else). In either case, the first matter of importance is your capacity for observation. As we stated earlier, observation will provide you with the material you need to develop the characters of your fictional stories.

Let's do some final exercises.

Exercise 32. Pause and thoroughly observe the way one walks, gesticulates, takes a glass, drinks water, and smokes ... Then when you are alone, try to imitate those movements. Don't do this in front of a mirror; do it for an imaginary onlooker.

Exercise 33. Do the same thing with an animal. Observe its movements and reactions very attentively and later try to imitate them for an imaginary onlooker.

Exercise 34. Perform the following actions: putting on your shoes and socks, washing and drying your hands and face, putting on make-up, or shaving. But do them without using socks, shoes, water, soap, a towel, cosmetics, or shaving accessories. Do them very carefully, however, concentrating all your attention on them. Don't be rushed and careless. Act as though you were really engaged in one of these daily activities. Re-create the activities with abundant detail and feel the weight, temperature, and texture of the objects.

Exercise 35. Look again at the outline of one of your chosen stories. Analyze one of the dialogues. Identify the characters participating in it, and try to establish their principal characteristics based on the logic of the story.

Go immediately to the following exercise.

Exercise 36. Stretch out comfortably on the floor or on your bed and gently close your eyes. As you did in the earlier exercises, relax and breathe slowly and deeply; begin to "review the film" of your story until you find yourself in the scene with the dialogue. Observe at length one character and then the other—how they speak and what gestures they make. Then introduce yourself into one of the characters, and from within him or her, observe at length the other speaker's gestures and actions. Then move into the second speaker and make the same observation about the first character. When you have finished, stand up without opening your eyes and begin to present that dialogue, passing from one character to the other and trying to speak, act, and make the same gestures as each of them does in your "film." When you finish, stretch out again on the floor or bed and move forward to the next dialogue, if there is one. Repeat this procedure until you have presented the last dialogue. Then stretch out again, breathe deeply and slowly open your eyes.

Go immediately to the next exercise.

Exercise 37. Retell the story to a chair or a broom. This time include your representation of the dialogues.

Don't forget to do these exercises with both of your selected stories.

Congratulations! You are now ready to tell your first two stories.

In the next chapter, you will find short, practical suggestions for the actual telling of a story. I suggest that you review them before you start telling in public. And then, with no more delays, seek the best opportunity to tell one of your two stories. It is a matter now of telling them over and over and of preparing others or choosing some from the last section of in this book, "Stories Ready to Tell." After you have told your story and evaluated the results, you can improve your quality as a teller. My advice is for you to keep an open mind and consider very seriously the spontaneous comments of your listeners, whether they are children or adults.

In a later chapter you will find new exercises to make your stories even more appealing. You must accept your "preparation" as an ongoing process with the never-ending possibility of learning something new.

CHAPTER FIVE

WHEN AND HOW TO TELL

The preceding chapters showed you how to prepare for telling your stories in an interesting and pleasurable way.

Now the time has come for you to tell your stories and to decide on how best to do so, given your audience and the setting you choose. I'm sure you remember that good tellers can tell the same story in very different ways, depending on the situation.

The circumstances in which storytelling occurs vary greatly, as do the ways in which stories are told. How a story is told differs depending on the social and cultural context and also on the artist's personality. Every storytelling performance is shaped by the personality of the teller and by the story itself, the location, the audience, and the atmosphere created. Clearly, there isn't just one, pre-established way of telling. Each time you tell a story, therefore, you'll have to find—or perhaps we should say, create—the most appropriate way. Some of the exercises you've done up to now will help you. You'll find it useful, however, to turn to the combination of general criteria and "tricks of the trade" in the following section, called "Practical Advice." Of course, there isn't any sense in memorizing them. I have only two suggestions: first, that you read them and reflect on them a little before telling the two first stories you have been working with; and, second, that you later reread them and reflect on them from time to time, in the light of your own experience as a teller.

The remaining sections of this chapter offer some ideas about using complementary resources such as puppets, masks, and music. These resources can embellish your stories and make them more appealing, while at the same time offering you new opportunities for creation and expression.

Practical Advice

To be a successful storyteller, you must, above all, feel calm and unhurried. We'll return to this topic later. For now, let's note that to tell a story in a way that satisfies your listeners, the first requirement is for you to feel an uncontrollable desire to tell it. This desire will shape your story, give it warmth and color, and provide that fountain of energy necessary for the story to "cast its spell." Don Porfirio, an extraordinary teller of hunting stories, used to tell me: "In order to tell, you have to put love into it. Everything is done with love. When you throw a stone, you have to do it with love; if not, it doesn't go well. The same thing happens with the story; without love it doesn't go well."

You'll also have to assess if the time is right for your audience. You don't want to select circumstances or social events at which people gather for some other purpose, like dancing, for example. It is true that in a rural environment, dances and wakes are favorite social events for tellers and their audiences. But stories are never told in the center of the dance area or alongside the deceased but rather outside, and the tellers take care not to bother those who aren't interested in the storytelling activity.

We can learn from them: you can tell stories at a party, but to one side, in an appropriate corner, unless everyone there wants to enjoy your stories.

Storytelling is an activity that requires deep concentration. You should also take care, therefore, that there are no external factors (especially noises and movements) that will distract the audience and interfere with their concentration. This factor is easier to control if your listeners—whether children or adults—are not present by chance but have been brought together specifically to enjoy stories since you can then put special care into selecting an adequate place, as acoustically isolated as possible. Not that you shouldn't tell stories, for example, in a park. I have done so many times. Some areas in a park are quieter than others, and the wind can be a great help if you put your back to it and use it to carry your voice toward the audience.

When you have a large audience, whether inside or outside, be sure that their seating arrangement makes it possible for you to establish direct eye contact with each of them. Usually a semicircle or horseshoe arrangement will do. Generally speaking, the rows should not extend too far back, but with experience you will come to your own conclusions. You can choose between telling while standing, seated or even lying down. My experience indicates that there are no rules in this regard. I generally tell my stories while standing, particularly when the audience is very large. I can be seen more easily; I can move around among the listeners; and it's easier for me to portray characters.

If you want to approach your storytelling with a sense of professionalism, you will need to pay attention to your attire and personal appearance. I have three recommendations in particular: wear simple clothes, if possible clothing without patterns or designs that can distract the audience; don't wear watches, jewelry or other objects that could interfere with the verisimilitude of your character portrayals; and if you have long hair, keep it pulled back so that it won't hide your face or constantly have to be pushed back.

Let's suppose that the moment has arrived and you find yourself seated on the edge of your child's bed, in front of some friends and family members in the living room or kitchen, or in a classroom. You may be aware of still another obstacle: the first few times you want to tell a story, you may discover that you're afraid to tell it. Perhaps you're afraid of not telling it well or of forgetting it, of the listeners' not liking it, or of making a fool of yourself. This fear is natural, and everyone experiences it, even the most famous professionals in storytelling and theater. Don't try to resist it because you will make matters worse. But don't spend too much time worrying about it, either. Just use it as the "driving force" of your story.

In reality, there isn't anything to fear. You aren't faced with giving the best storytelling performance in the world. You're simply going to tell your story, a story that you have carefully selected and that you know very well, as well as if it had happened to you. All you have to do is to start telling it, and then it will flow naturally, just as when you come home and tell about what happened to you during the day. But something more is at play here: it is as if something "incredible" happened to you during the day and you're putting all your effort into making your listeners believe it. This effort will be reflected in the "convinced-convincing" look on your face and in your gestures and body expression, even when you don't use these communication techniques on purpose. What I ought to say here is that you must not use them on purpose. Instead, be natural and sincere; concentrate on your objective, namely, to share a story that you and all those present believe in. That is all. Then your attitude will be "natural," the way it is when some extraordinary event has happened to you.

You can also turn to an old professional trick: before beginning the story, you can "break the ice" by telling an anecdote, asking the audience questions, talking about whatever seems appropriate at that moment,

When and How to Tell

or telling a joke or a very short story. Any of these recourses can be useful for breaking the ice, in other words, for measuring the reaction of the audience and simultaneously bolstering your self-confidence. We remember that the *kodanshi*—those magnificent Japanese tellers who specialize in telling important historical events—often pave the way by telling a joke, talking about the weather, or commenting on the result of sports match.

At first you'll probably tend to rush through your telling, trying to finish quickly and be done with those nervous feelings that most likely you won't have under complete control, and maybe you're even afraid of taking too much of your listeners' time. Don't rush; don't tell in a hurried fashion. Take delight in your emotional state; it is your involvement that enables your listeners to see and feel things at that moment that they otherwise wouldn't be able to. So, don't rush yourself in any way. Each image needs its time: first, so that you can see and feel it; second, so that you can convey it; and lastly, so that your audience can re-create it and enjoy it as well. Remember: don't rush yourself. Each moment of the story is marvelous and very precious.

There are two errors frequently made by novice tellers that I recommend you avoid. First, except for suitably chosen exceptions, don't introduce your story by giving its title and author (if you have that information). Otherwise, in his imagination the listener is sent to an object called a "book" instead of being transported to the time and/or ambiance in which the story takes place. Second, don't offer any information that will let your audience anticipate how your story will develop or how it will end. This kind of forewarning can cause listeners to lose interest.

Before you begin, close your eyes for an instant and immerse yourself in the story. Visualize it in its entirety. Let yourself be filled with its sensations and images. Then, while you're telling, make eye contact with your listeners unless some cultural convention, the absence of light, or the development of the story makes it unadvisable. Entice them to listen attentively. Let all the love that you feel for them flow through the story. Don't hesitate to enter into physical contact with your audience while you are telling. If there are no social conventions that discourage it, physical contact will not bother your listeners; on the contrary, they will appreciate it. And remember, tell slowly and take pleasure in it.

That pleasure will be a key element in making your storytelling a success. Indeed, the teller's attitude is a force that shapes his performance. So, if you enjoy it, others will enjoy it. Forget about yourself; don't seek to excel but rather to share, to give. The teller is an individual who possesses and who gives. He possesses a story and wants to share it: that is why he is appreciated. But he is even more appreciated for his ability to share it with freshness, enthusiasm, and vitality. It is important to know how to read your audience in order to establish a connection, a communion, with them. You will soon see that if you forget something, you will accept the oversight in a calm, natural way, and thanks to your ability to improvise, you'll be able to resolve the problem without the audience's even noticing.

In order to improvise, it isn't enough to know the story well and have a vivid imagination. You must also have a good vocabulary, so make a permanent commitment to increasing it. Enjoy each word; savor it; yes, relish it. You will have to choose your words carefully, however. Avoid pretentious or grandiloquent words. You don't want your descriptions of the characters or the setting too precise or limiting; you want them open and evocative. Some of the recommendations offered to writers by the master writer Horacio Quiroga in his *Ten Rules for the Perfect Storyteller* are extremely valuable for oral storytellers. Let us note numbers six and seven:

6. If you want to express with precision that "A cold wind was blowing from the river," there are no other words in human language to express it.

7. Use no adjectives unless they are necessary. So many tails stuck on to a weak noun will be useless. If you find the right adjective, its hue will be incomparable. But you have to find it.

If you're telling to children, refrain from abusing diminutives, talking in a child's voice, or pondering about the "edifying" value of your telling. These distortions, which adults frequently commit when their listeners are children, are so serious that they diminish any telling.

You'll want to resist relying on clichéd repetitions and instead increase your use of a variety of connectives to link the events being narrated in your story. You should avoid constantly repeating the over-worked word "so." There are many adverbs and adverbial phrases that can indicate the succession of events when used appropriately: examples are *then, later, at that moment, afterwards, immediately, quickly,* and *all at once.* There are other connectives for expressing the type of relation that links events: *on the other hand, consequently, in spite of, therefore, still,* and *since,* for instance. By the same token, don't put all objects simply "here" or "there"; other possibilities include *behind, in front of, below, above, under, over, on top of, between, at the end, at the beginning,* and *alongside.*

When the story includes dialogues, try to differentiate the characters' voices and gestures; there have already been some exercises for developing this skill, and others will follow. Don't hesitate to utilize an everyday object to represent something from the story and even to "animate" it as if it were a puppet representing a character; you will find some exercises and specific recommendations for developing this technique later in this chapter. Rest assured that your portrayal of scenes from the story will be appreciated. Proceed with confidence and let your body be guided by your imagination. Any object, natural phenomenon, or character that you put on stage must occupy that exact same space in your mental visualization. Otherwise you risk such a lapse as putting an elephant on stage in your audience's imagination and shortly afterwards walking over it as if it didn't exist. This slip-up would be noticed by many listeners and would make it difficult—or at the very least, less interesting—for them to follow your story.

Onomatopoeias are usually another great resource for a good teller, who not only uses the traditional ones but typically creates others, depending on his tastes and needs. Onomatopoeia is a simplified representation of real sounds, and its use has a special, magical effect. Invent the ones you need, and when you pronounce them, try to savor this act of verbal "trickery." Give these representations your own special flavor and enjoy producing them.

Don't forget, however, that the principal resources of any teller are voice and body expressiveness, from the head down to the toes. You'll find relevant information and exercises in the next chapter. Use these resources to their greatest advantage. As you practice your story, you'll discover new possibilities for expressing yourself and being creative. Keep in mind that you can create an imaginary world with your voice through variations in volume, tone (high-pitched vs. deep), texture (a greater or lesser degree of breathiness) and rhythm. Silences are also a very powerful instrument; it is essential to know how to use them at the right moment. You can use your body and facial expression to emphasize them.

When you've finished telling the story, don't suddenly separate yourself from your audience. You've built a bridge that they now will want to cross with gestures of affection, stories of personal experiences, or other methods for forging a closer relationship. In your performance as a teller you can't neglect this aspect. It's even more important if you're telling for social or educational purposes; you must be very attentive to these situations.

Don't forget that each person tells in his or her own way. Telling is an art; it is an expressive and creative activity. The manner of telling, therefore, depends strongly on the teller's personality and circumstances. Don't let yourself be unduly influenced by any type of "instructions," even those which I myself, without wanting to, have allowed to peek out from these pages. When you tell, let your soul come out. Perhaps this instruction is the only truly good one.

Puppets, Masks, Costumes and Other Props

Musicians, puppeteers, and actors—in addition to parents, teachers, organizers of cultural events, and other specialists—are among those who customarily attend my storytelling courses. Some of them are afraid of "mixing" the arts, and they often ask me if it is acceptable to include in their stories some of the resources they use in their creative disciplines. I have always told them that they must develop their expression and creativity as they themselves think best.

I'll go even farther, however, and say that I believe that tellers should use their own personal inclinations and abilities to the greatest possible benefit. If you already use one or more of these resources, therefore, don't hesitate to incorporate them into your storytelling. If you don't use them but would like to, then start using them; it will be to your advantage to do so. In any case, there isn't much sense or benefit in limiting creative possibilities to already established and separate forms of art such as theater, music, dance, or storytelling.

This brief section and the two that follow are addressed to readers who don't have any experience in these areas, and my focus will be on the possibilities of using certain complementary resources. I don't claim to offer a course on puppets, masks and costumes or an introduction to music. I am only offering ideas on how to incorporate these types of resources into storytelling.

Supplementary objects, or props, are a resource that tellers in rural areas often turn to. For them, the use of such objects depends more on chance circumstances than on a decision made beforehand. There are no rules on whether or not such resources can be used. Some professional tellers from the cities make extensive, planned use of objects and costumes; others, in contrast, renounce this type of resource "on principle." I myself cultivate both styles.

There are objects that can serve as props without being specifically designed for that purpose. Let's consider, for example, how we can use a handkerchief. A handkerchief can be a puppet if it is handled right and if "life" is breathed into it. You might find it helpful to use one to portray a character from your story. Great puppeteers insist that a puppet doesn't have to be a doll; in principle, they say, a puppet is an "animate object." So, animate the handkerchief; endow it with life. How are you going to do this? Begin by assuming that it really is the character. It can be an excellent aid for portraying a ghost, for example. If you truly make the handkerchief come to life, if you feel and act as though it were alive, you will probably make your audience believe it, too. The art of storytelling, like that of theater and puppetry, rests on a convention: in all three arts, the performers act "as if," and if they are truly consistent in their performance, they succeed in making their audience accept the "as if" as well. Of course, this "as if" is different in each of these arts, but it is found in all three of them.

You can also improvise a versatile costume element from a handkerchief. Let me to return to the story of Little Red Riding Hood. Be it white, yellow, or polka-dotted, a handkerchief placed on your head like a shawl will suggest the presence of Little Red Riding Hood. Meanwhile, without any other accessory, you would be the narrator and, by changing your voice and body expression, you could portray the wolf as well. You could choose another object for portraying the wolf if you wanted to, but note that you could employ that same handkerchief just by using it in a different way. Two alternatives occur to me: you could tie the handkerchief at your neck like a napkin, in humorous reference to the known outcome of the story, or you could stretch it tightly across your face like a mask, imparting an

When and How to Tell

evil, mysterious air to the character. The same handkerchief could later be used as the grandmother's nightcap should you want the challenge of using a single object to distinguish all three characters. The challenge could be an interesting one.

Let me emphasize that the success of any of these alternatives depends on you and not on the handkerchief. The handkerchief will be a prop, an object onto which to project the force of your imagination in order to help define the character in question. Since the object is serving as a puppet, a hood, a napkin, a mask, or a nightcap to enhance character portrayal, all the comments about character portrayal in previous chapters are valid. For example, each character must have a clear and unequivocal place in the storytelling space. One character in a dialogue turns his face from the left toward the center and the other from the right toward the center, since both characters cannot be in the same place at the same time. Your audience would immediately notice if they were, and this misstep would spoil your performance. You could also make one character taller than the other, but we aren't going to settle for this kind of differentiation. The characters have to have different voices and body expression.

Let's return to the example of the ghost portrayed with a suitably handled handkerchief. Now try to give it a voice and make it seem that the voice is coming from the handkerchief. In other words, you won't speak with your face to the audience; you could put the hand that is holding the puppet or your forearm in front of your face and let your body, which won't be concealed like that of the usual puppeteer, respond creatively to this circumstance. If wouldn't make any sense for you to remain in one position, either standing or seated, and act as if nothing were happening, as if the ghost weren't there. To do so would diminish the effect of all your play in animating the object, that is, the handkerchief-become-ghost.

The same thing can be said about using the handkerchief as a costume element. With it placed on your head, you have a conventional portrayal of Little Red Riding Hood, but that won't be enough. The handkerchief on your head should become the pretext for developing a Little Red Riding Hood with her own voice and characteristic movements. It will be very interesting when the wolf appears, and the contrast between their voices and body movements will be appreciated. There will be a contrast, of course, since you can't merely cover your face with the handkerchief to portray "the evil one"; you will have to develop appropriate voice and body expression for the wolf, too. By the same token, you can't portray "the glutton" just by putting the handkerchief around your neck as if it were a napkin; facial expressions and movements of the eyes and hands and probably the tongue as well will have to play an important role.

I venture to say that everything will flow very naturally from your inner being if you simply let it happen, that is, if you don't judge yourself beforehand and don't allow yourself to be "blackmailed" by the fear of looking ridiculous. Please note that I use the word "naturally" on purpose. I use it because for a very long time and among all the peoples of the world, masks, dolls, and costumes have been a stimulus for human beings to set free the boundless imaginary characters that they carry within them. This statement is corroborated by the works on theater and dramatic play, on psychology in general, and on psychodrama in particular that are found in the specialized bibliography at the back of the book; you can verify it yourself, however, just by observing the play of children or adults at a masquerade party.

There is one other use for the handkerchief that we chose as an object for illustration—it could be an actual handkerchief that you have in your hand. It could have been found at the scene of the crime, or it could have belonged to some famous person, or it could bear some particular mark, like a bloodstain, that will be revealed only at the end and that will explain the meaning of the story. There are many things that you can do with a handkerchief or other prop. Just remember that the object itself does not resolve anything in the story; it merely provides you, the storyteller, with a concrete point of reference for resolving things yourself.

My experience with a story about a stone told by Mano Cola, a Venezuelan rural teller from the Andean region, can serve as a good example of how the object itself isn't what is important; what is important is the relationship that the teller establishes with the object and through it, with his audience. The holidays of San Isidro Labrador had ended, and my party and I were in the town square with Mano Cola and his neighbors, talking and telling stories. It started getting very cold, and Mano Cola invited us to his house to show us "a stone that was growing." We went to his home and made ourselves comfortable in a room at the front of the house, next to a window. Mano Cola gave us some preliminary, intriguing information about the stone—he said that not only was it growing but that the image of the Virgin Mary was inside it. Then he left the room to get the stone. When he returned, he was carrying in his hand a package so small that it could have fit inside his fist. He began to untie it slowly. A candle wick was wrapped around the package several times, and there were quite a few sheets of paper. While he was untying and unwrapping it, carefully keeping his eyes on his work, he told us how he had obtained this marvelous stone and how the parish priest had assured him that it "was growing." He took several minutes, and during that time, with his assured, calm manner and the tone, texture, and rhythm of his voice, he created an atmosphere of mystery that drew in all of us. So, when that fantastic piece of quartz finally appeared in the palm of his hand, we all rushed forward to examine it. Mano Cola handed the stone to the oldest of his neighbors, who examined it carefully against the light. Then it was passed from hand to hand; we all sought the angle that would allow us to marvel at seeing inside it what indeed seemed to be the figure of the Virgin seated on a rock. The story deeply impressed me, and despite my skepticism, I felt that Mano Cola had totally involved me in his mystery. Days later, when I left the village, I did so convinced that while the stone itself was perhaps not an extraordinary phenomenon, it had been my good fortune to take part in a most extraordinary moment of storytelling involving an object.

Let me emphasize that Mano Cola's voice, its nuances, his conviction, and thus his assured and solemn attitude were very important in this telling. I also need to point out that, unlike what would more often be the case, he at no time looked at us; his eyes remained fixed on the object of his story, compelling us to look at it, too, and thus "validating the object," as one usually says in theater.

To sum up, physical objects can be used for various purposes and can greatly enhance a storytelling performance. The objects themselves won't make the telling a success, however; the teller must transform them into elements that support and enrich the performance. Of course, the objects don't have to be informal like those we used as examples; they can be specifically designed and constructed for the story. They can also be ready-made puppets or masks. Obviously, a beautifully made puppet or mask is preferable to one that is carelessly made. But as used here, the term "beautifully made" is not synonymous with "mass-produced"; our interest is in the object's expressive power. Depending on the cultural standards of your surroundings, on your story, and on your way of telling it, expressive power may or may not require careful crafting and may or may not be present in a mass-produced item. In principle, I myself am not inclined to use ready-made objects, and though I have turned to them with satisfactory results, I prefer puppets and masks that either I or people who work closely with me have made. I suggest that you give making your own objects a try.

It is different with how you dress. If you don't know how to sew, then creating a costume can be a frustrating task. Think about making a jacket or a hat, and you will see what I mean.

When and How to Tell

Recycling old family clothes or buying clothes in antique sales could be the best solution. Since costume elements notably enhance storytelling, the effort is well worth your while. The principle already suggested with regard to puppets, masks, and costume accessories (like the hood, nightcap and napkin) remains the same: a costume doesn't make your portrayal of a character a success; it serves to support you as you yourself make the portrayal a success.

On the other hand, what you wear can depict the characters in the story and establish your presence as the storyteller as well. Earlier we advocated dressing in some "neutral" way, but certain types of stories or audiences can suggest, and even require, other solutions, which you will have to assess when the opportunity arises. As the teller, for example, you can be an old hunter, a sailor, or a traveler who comes from far away. It will depend on the kinds of stories you foresee for the occasion and on your interest in adopting a persona that isn't your own. As for using costumes in the portrayal of characters from a story, I am of the opinion that costuming shouldn't be overdone. First of all, you risk depriving audience members of the opportunity to imagine a character in their own way, and let us remember that one of the major attractions of the art of storytelling lies in its ability to give free rein to the listeners' imagination. I find it preferable, therefore, to draw on clothing that merely suggests or evokes a character. Moreover, there is a practical factor that discourages excessive costuming. As the teller, you have to be yourself and, in addition, represent each one of your characters without interrupting the flow of the story; it is impossible, therefore, for you to make major changes in clothing when moving from one role to another. On the contrary, if you opt for incorporating costumes into your story, you should use only one item of clothing to portray a given character, and it will have to be something easily slipped on and off. When the moment has come to depict another character engaged in the conversation, you want to put something else on or perhaps pick up some object without missing a beat.

Pictures

In principle, I believe that in the pursuit of creativity, everything has merit. But I believe this only "in principle." Before you put a specific idea into practice, it is wise to reflect on it and give thought to what characterizes it and what its possible effects are. There is a certain type of storytelling that I find unsuitable, and I want to point it out explicitly because it is very widespread in schools. I am speaking of storytelling with pictures.

In many of my courses I have had librarians and teachers—particularly those who specialize in children of pre-school-age—who have been taught that stories should be told with pictures. They have generally joined my courses convinced that this approach is the best way to tell a story, but they soon change their minds and decide not to use that method at all.

This type of storytelling usually ranges between holding an open book or a picture in one hand while reading or telling the story and, at the other extreme, having pictures in the room and pointing to the appropriate picture while telling the story. The usual justification for this form of storytelling is that it allows the children to learn the words they don't know and still follow the narrative thread. It should be noted, however, that even when it is true that the children don't know all the vocabulary used, this simplistic solution has very negative results. It is simplistic because it tries "to kill two birds with one stone" without reflecting on the nature of the pedagogical technique and its consequences. Showing pictures or projecting slides can indeed be a valuable way to use visual images in order to familiarize children with some elements of reality and, consequently, increase their vocabulary. Storytelling, however, is a completely different matter. I find nothing wrong with applying the art of storytelling to pedagogical objectives; on the contrary, I believe that we should make the most of the application of storytelling and other arts in the schools. However, if we are to guarantee children a suitable sensory experience as well as achieve our desired pedagogical objectives in the most effective way, we have to base the application of storytelling on the recognition that it is an art. I will discuss storytelling applications in the next chapter. In the meantime, let's look for constructive solutions to the problem repeatedly raised by the practice of telling stories with pictures.

If we want children to enjoy hearing a story that may include words they don't know, then the solution is to familiarize them with the meaning and visual representation of the words in advance. With suitable planning of classroom activities, this objective can be accomplished through pictures, photographs, or field trips. If you choose to use pictures to familiarize the children with the appropriate visual images, it won't be enough merely to show them. You will have to talk about what is represented in them. Of course, your talk can't be reduced to a monotonous repetition of the given word; it has to be transformed into creative, playful speech that the children find appealing and that effectively uses the words in question by finding ways to apply them. Applying them through telling a story, however, isn't the answer: doing that would destroy the story's magic and at the same time encourage children to associate a story with a lesson. As a result, their ability to enjoy the art of storytelling, and, by extension, literature, would be negatively affected.

On the other hand, if it is a question of older children or if there are only a few unfamiliar words that can be understood in the narrative context, then it wouldn't be necessary to show pictures beforehand. It is better for children to be stimulated to exercise their imagination and infer the meaning of words through context, just as they will often have to do as adults. In any event, the meanings can be worked on later or pictures can be shown after the story is told. I stated above that the magic of a story would be destroyed because the exercise of imagination through stimulation by word, or by word and gesture, or by word, gesture and object (not a picture) would be inhibited; instead, the version of the picture or photograph shown would shape the listener's image of the character, situation, or setting in question. If there is an elephant in the story, for example, the child will "see" only the elephant he is now being shown; he will be deprived of the opportunity to create his own image by drawing on elephants or pictures of them that he may have seen in the past.

There is a more serious effect: if the teacher has to point to a picture and the children have to look at it, then the relationship between teller and audience is broken, and this relationship, as we have seen, is an essential element in the art of storytelling. Moreover, there will be no change in the stereotypical relationship of "teacher who instructs—student who learns."

4. Singing, Music and Sound Effects

I said earlier that there is nothing undesirable about combining the arts and putting your abilities and talents to good use. I find this especially true in the case of singing and music. They can be an enhancement to storytelling, and the same can be said of sound effects. Here are some suggestions for using these resources:

- The teller hums or softly sings some melody that is unique to a specific character or that conveys the atmosphere of the story's setting.
- The teller sings a song as part of the story, accompanied or not by an instrument played either by the teller or by another person.
- The same teller (or an assistant or assistants suitably informed in advance—see the next section entitled "Participation") produces sound effects with his voice, by slapping his hands on various parts

of his body, by stomping his feet on the floor, or by utilizing a whole range of objects, including musical instruments.
- At the appropriate moment, the teller or an assistant plays a previously taped soundtrack with music or special effects.

These are valid possibilities for embellishing a story if they are suitably used. Let me caution you, however, that whichever of the above possibilities you choose, you should avoid abusing the resource if you want it to enhance your telling. Special care must be given to the use of tape recordings. First of all, since a storyteller can freely improvise his pace, there is little reason to recommend playing a tape with pre-programmed effects. It could happen that the sounds would cut in at the wrong time or that the teller would have to change his narrative rhythm to accommodate them. The recording could be played at a precise moment, but the sound effects should only accompany or serve as the background for some action that the teller performs. Of course, there are exceptions—which one should always be ready to consider and even deliberately invent—but, in principle, it seems ill-advised to replace active portrayal in storytelling with mechanical sound.

Active Audience Participation

One of the distinguishing features of the art of storytelling is the close, interactive relationship between teller and audience. Some tellers are extremely conscious of it, while others are less so; all of them, however, greatly profit from it. In any case, all tellers who give a live performance establish a close contact with their audience, regardless of the mode that the audience adopts.

In a certain sense, the listeners always participate. At the very least they do so with the activity of their imagination. But we are going to discuss an obvious mode of participation that is visible to everyone present. I've decided to call it "active" to distinguish it from the other type of participation, though I'm aware that using one's imagination also presupposes an activity.

The audience's active participation can be deliberately stimulated by the teller or it can be spontaneous. In the first case, the type of stimulation that the teller provides will to some degree structure the audience's participation. In the second, anything can happen, be it good or bad. Once audience participation manifests itself, the teller has no choice but to do something with it. Theoretically, he can choose from among the following possibilities: let it develop freely, play with it, direct it, or repress it. Depending on the circumstances, on the teller's personality, and on the type of audience, I think that almost all combinations are valid, except in the following cases: if the participation has been spontaneous and in turn remains totally free to develop as it will, it can happen that the teller has to stop performing. It is better for tellers to be aware of this possibility and at least be disposed to play with audience participation if for some reason they prefer not to direct it. On the other hand, if a teller puts a stop to the participation, no matter whether he stimulated it or not, the audience can lose interest and even be upset.

But all the other possibilities are valid. The decision will depend on whether you are telling simply for aesthetic pleasure, recreation, or expression or whether you have the purpose of application in mind. For right now we will leave the matter of application to one side, since a separate chapter is dedicated to it. The ways to stimulate, direct, or play with audience participation vary greatly, depending on the narrator, the audience, and the circumstances before, during, or after each story. Nonetheless, I can suggest that you evaluate the techniques offered below, and, of course, come up with your own.

- Ask questions of the audience as a whole, collect the answers, and then play with them. You can use the questions to introduce

When and How to Tell

the subject before you tell the story, and you can also use them during the telling to have the audience make decisions about the characters. In keeping with the input of the audience, you could then do one or both of the following activities: change the course of the story or have your listeners discuss aspects of the story as it is changed.

- After the story is told, use questions to encourage the audience to briefly share personal experiences similar to events in the story.
- Invite the entire audience (or organize it into groups) to produce sound effects during the story; with as few instructions as possible, clearly establish beforehand how the participation is to take place.
- Invite the audience (or some members) to participate in dramatizing certain characters; again, with as few instructions as possible, clearly establish beforehand how the participation is to take place.
- Encourage the audience to sing with you, to chant, and to mark the rhythm; as before, first clearly establish, with as few instructions as possible, how the participation is to take place.
- Without prior warning, engage members of the audience in dialogue during the story, either in your role as teller or as a character you are portraying (in the latter case, put your spectator in the position of the other character with whom you are conversing).
- Be sure in advance that this interaction will be readily accepted and that the spectator will know how to respond.
- Without prior warning, interact physically with members of the audience. Be sure that they will accept this interaction.
- Convert a spectator into a "puppet" who is manipulated and whose voice you produce or whom you "cue" so that a character from the story is portrayed. Again, be certain beforehand of your spectator's acceptance and response.

- Encourage, as part of the story, the audience's participation in an activity (for example, dances, dramatizations, and playing with balls, strings, or pieces of cloth).
- Ask the audience to suggest characters and situations for a story that you and they will then construct together.

The list could go on. The suggestions I've given you include those which I've used successfully and in which both children and adults have enthusiastically participated.

There is no doubt that these are the essential factors: appropriately choosing the circumstances and type of stimuli and direction you will provide; your own disposition as participant or "player"; your confidence in your skill to direct an activity; and the clarity of the instructions for participation. But what is especially important is your ability to resolve the situation if you make an error. To deal with this possible occurrence, it will be very helpful to make use of the earlier recommendations for developing your ability to improvise.

Finally, you should avoid promoting the hysterical, unthinking and manipulative participation that some televisions programs have made fashionable with today's public and that is gradually invading the field of children's theater as well as the work of clowns and television hosts of children's festivities. I am referring to that participation in which everyone mindlessly jumps and shouts at the same time, repeating a couple of words introduced by the director and responding in chorus to silly questions. If you are going to encourage audience participation, you should assume that your audience members are as intelligent and as sensitive as you are and that they deserve your love and respect. Let me share something more with you from my own experience: it is possible that some participants will be influenced by the above-mentioned type of "hysterical, unthinking and manipulative" participation. Should that happen, you will have to make it clear that your style of direction is different and, if it occurs spontaneously, you will have to redirect it toward a positive type of participation.

Formulaic Beginnings, Endings, and Invitations for Others to Tell

The most widespread formulas for beginning and ending a story today are, respectively, "Once upon a time" and "And now my story has ended." There are other formulas, and you can also start your story immediately, without any type of characteristic formula, and you can finish it in your own way. In any case, you will find below a list of some formulaic expressions from different oral traditions along with some of my own creation. I offer them for you to use with complete freedom, but above all I encourage you to invent your own.

Beginnings

- This is an old story …
- Many years ago, when neither you nor I had been born, it happened that …
- Long ago, when the world was still being formed …
- Long ago, when the world was still being formed and the animals still could talk …
- Long ago, when chickens had teeth …
- Long ago, when pigs still wore hats …
- Long ago, when cats wore shoes …
- In the days when the world was beginning, it happened that …

- Before our time, in a country far away, even farther than …
- Once my great grandmother walked and walked, she walked all that she could, week after week, month after month, year after year, until she arrived at a faraway town where …
- Once my great grandmother told me that she went far away, very far away, even farther than I could explain and then …
- There was once …
- It was a …
- Once upon a time in an old country …
- The old people in North Africa say that …
- My grandmother always used to tell me that there in …
- Although you will find it hard to believe …
- You can also begin stories with questions that focus on the kind of events that you're going to relate or on a character, such as: "Did you know that …?", "Do you believe that …?", or "Has anybody ever seen a …?"
- It can be a lot of fun to begin with pre-established interaction formulas. For example, the teller says, "Crick", to which the audience responds "Crack." This is done several times in a crescendo until the teller decides that it is time to begin the story. Clearly, the first time it is used, the audience has to be informed about the pattern of response. (The use of this formula has been reported on various islands of the Caribbean, among the sailors of Upper Brittany, and among indigenous peoples of North America, as we mentioned in an earlier chapter).

Endings

- Coppery Colorado, this story must stop; it passed along one road and then down another, but tomorrow for sure I'll tell you another.

- Listen! The rooster has crowed, and my story is told.
- And this story has ended.
- And whoosh, whoosh, this story was carried off by the wind.
- The story has come to an end and been carried off by the wind.
- If only you knew how much I regret that my story has drawn to a close.
- Pelen-pen-pen we've come to the end.
- They lived happily ever after and ate scallops and snapper.
- And they lived in contentment and told each other stories every day.

Inviting Others to Tell

- Whether true or whether invented, tell your story for mine has ended.
- The river is narrow, and the sea is wide; tell your story for I've told mine.
- I've told my story and so I'm done; now it's your turn to tell me one.
- My story was a lullaby for you; and now I'd like to hear yours, too.
- My story left by one road and returned by a second; now it's your story that steps up and beckons.
- And thus it ended, and then the wind blew, and now for a story I'll listen to you.
- It went over the mountain and crossed the sea, and now it's your turn to tell to me.
- To hear your tale would be a privilege, for I've walked down the river and come to a bridge.

How to Tell Stories: A Latin American Perspective

CHAPTER SIX

EXERCISES FOR IMPROVING YOUR TELLING AND FOR ORGANIZING A BASIC STORYTELLING WORKSHOP

The exercises in the first four chapters have already helped you develop the skills you need to begin telling stories successfully and enjoyably. Chapter Five contained information for making this success and enjoyment even greater. What is best for you to do now is to tell, tell, and tell some more, learning everything you can from the experience. In this chapter, I'll offer more exercises for developing your abilities and resources as a teller. These exercises have a second possible use. Once you've spent time telling stories and reflecting on this art, you could organize a basic workshop to help others learn the art of storytelling. You would rely on your own sensitivity and creative experience, of course, but you should also search out information about educational strategies that are appropriate to your new role as workshop leader. You will find some basic texts in the bibliography. In the meantime, you may find it interesting to consider some fundamental principles that guide my educative work. I'll express them as follows: not teaching but rather humbly helping the participants to learn; understanding that activities are focused solely on the participants, not on the leader; not believing that the seed of an art is sown in the learners, for that seed is already there and one only helps to develop it; not proposing that the learners tell in the same way as the leader but rather guiding them to find their own personal style; and being alert to the natural tendency of some learners to imitate the "teacher's" style and surreptitiously putting an end to it.

Since several people participate in a workshop, group exercises are especially useful. Although the exercises included here can be done in a group, they have also been designed for a teller to do alone at home or in any small space.

1. Breathing

In addition to being a key factor for enjoying good health, proper breathing results in better voice emission. The emission of vocal sound is impossible without the current of air that produces it; since the voice plays such an important role in telling, you'll want to have a large volume of air at your disposal so that you can better control your speech production.

Exercise 1. Lie on your back on the floor or any hard surface. Stretch your arms and legs out. Make certain that your hands are open and that there is no tension in any part of your body. Inhaling only through your nose, breathe slowly, deeply, and silently. At the same time, let the column of air pass to the lower part of your lungs by relaxing the abdomen and expanding the diaphragm; keep your shoulders in their original position and don't dilate or raise the thorax. To exhale, open your mouth half the way, gently extend your lips forward, and expel the air while slowly contracting the diaphragm. Exhale slowly and silently. Let all the air out of your lungs and inhale again.

Exercise 2. Keep the same position as for Exercise 1. Inhale the same way you did in that exercise, but now count mentally to six while you inhale. Keep the air in your lungs with the diaphragm expanded while you again count to six. Exhale as before, breathing out to a count of six. Let all the air out of your lungs and repeat the procedure.

Exercise 3. Do the same as in Exercise 2, but count to ten in each instance.

Exercise 4. Lie down in the same position as for the previous exercises. Begin inhaling the same way. When you feel that you have expanded the diaphragm almost as far as you can and have almost filled the lower part of the lungs with air, continue inhaling and let the air enter and remain in the upper part of the lungs; dilate the thorax slowly as the air is entering. Prolong this inhaling to a count of six. Then keep it in your lungs while your mentally count to six. Finally, exhale for the same amount of time. While exhaling, open your mouth half way and begin to expel the air while compressing the diaphragm, first dislodging the air from the lower part of the lungs and then from the upper part. Let all the air out of your lungs and inhale again.

Exercise 5. Do the same as for Exercise 4, but count to ten.

Do this series of five exercises without interruption. It would be ideal to spend some 3–5 minutes on each of them. While you are doing them, try to be conscious of the muscles involved in breathing and particularly of the movement of the diaphragm.

Exercise 6. Do Exercise 5, but open your mouth wide and exhale for a count of ten, maintaining the same force and volume of expelled air throughout the count.

Exercise 7. Do the same as for Exercise 6, but with your mouth somewhat less opened and the lips extended out more. Imagine that you are pushing a light object with the expelled air.

Exercise 8. Do the same as for Exercise 6, but do it while you're walking. Remember that here as in all the other exercises, both your inhaling and exhaling are very slow and silent and—thanks to the mental count—controlled and uniform.

2. Preparing the Sound Production System

The following exercises for preparing your sound production system are similar in a way to the warm-up exercises a professional athlete does before playing a sport. You won't need to do them if you are going to tell in front of a small group of people in a small, enclosed area. On the other hand, you must prepare your voice for a major effort if you want it to serve your creative intentions and not suffer physiological damage. Classroom teachers regularly speak a great deal, and since they don't receive vocal training during their professional preparation, many of them often have serious problems with their voice. Practicing the following exercises constitutes a basic preventive plan for avoiding these problems. Vocal emission is strongly associated with breathing. You can see, therefore, that the initial preparatory exercises are the very same breathing exercises of the preceding section. While good vocal emission is possible only in a general state of relaxation, it is particularly important that the organs directly involved be relaxed. There is nothing more damaging for the organism and disagreeable for the audience than the excessive, counterproductive effort made when a teller tenses up his vocal cords, tongue, or jaw. The tension will immediately be revealed in the teller's neck, and the audience will notice it at once.

Below are suggestions for some exercises to relax and prepare the muscles of your sound production system.

Exercise 1: Roll your head gently in a circle, relaxing the neck. Do it very gently and slowly, each time trying to draw a wider circle, letting

Exercises for Improving Your Telling and for Organizing a Basic Storytelling

your head fall toward your back when it moves toward the nape of your neck, letting it fall toward the chest when the chin moves forward, and pointing the temples toward the corresponding shoulder when it moves to the sides. Repeat this movement some ten or fifteen times, first in a clockwise, and then in a counterclockwise direction.

Exercise 2: Yawn several times with exaggeration.

Exercise 3: Make chewing movements, imagining that you have a huge wad of gum in your mouth. Open your mouth wide, and each time close it tightly. Do these actions some ten or fifteen times.

Exercise 4: Open your mouth and stick your tongue out quickly and energetically, as if you were a lizard catching an insect. Repeat this exercise ten to fifteen times.

Exercise 5: Massage your palette with the upper surface of your tongue. Do it slowly but with intense pressure. Repeat this action ten to fifteen times.

Exercise 6: Rest the end of your tongue on any point of your lips and run your tongue completely around your lips until you return to the starting point. Keep the end of the tongue within the line of your lips. Do this exercise slowly. Repeat it ten to fifteen times while moving your tongue in one direction, and ten to fifteen times in the other direction.

Exercise 7: Inhale as you learned to do in the breathing exercises in the preceding section and begin to exhale. After a brief instant, stop the free exhaling and convert it into one that produces the sound "aah," prolonging it like a long sigh. Repeat this exercise ten to fifteen times.

Exercise 8: Inhale and begin to exhale as you did in the previous exercise. This time, instead of interrupting the free exhalation with the emission of "aah," you will gently close your lips, thus effortlessly producing the sound of a prolonged "m." Observe how the bony parts of your head vibrate.

Do this exercise ten to fifteen times. Be careful not to try to produce the sound of the "m" deliberately but to let it happen as the result of your closing your lips very softly.

Exercise 9: Inhale as you did in the preceding exercise but this time, instead of exhaling freely, say a prolonged "aah." Repeat the exercise with the rest of the vowels. Open your mouth wide.

3. Developing Vocal Expression

You should do the exercises in this section after finishing those in the preceding section so that your sound production organs are properly prepared.

Stand facing a bare wall. Throughout all the exercises you will stay there, only one step away from the wall. Keep your feet apart at a distance equal to the width between your shoulders. Keep your back naturally straight and relaxed. Let your arms fall to the sides of your body. The head is held high and is relaxed; keep your eyes directed toward the wall. You should feel comfortable in the position just assumed; if not, vary it as you do the exercises.

Exercise 1: Say any one of the vowels as you did in Exercise 9 in the previous section. This time, however, do not say it in a continuous, prolonged manner; instead, open and close your mouth freely, varying the duration and volume of the vocal emission. Let the tone, the texture, and, in general, all the characteristics of your voice be modified freely in response to the following imaginary stimuli: let your voice softly caress the wall; after a while go to another vowel and let your voice tickle it; go to another vowel and penetrate the wall with your voice; go to another and frighten it; go to another and seduce it.

Exercise 2: Follow the instructions for the previous exercise, but this time, while you are saying the vowels, make the following associations: pressing, pulling, pushing, twisting, and stretching the wall.

Exercise 3: Follow the instructions for Exercise 1, this time not voicing a vowel but any type of sound that you wish. Make that same wall feel the following in succession: a breeze, a rain, a downpour, a storm, a hurricane, a tiger lying in wait, the purring of a cat, a melody, or some other image that you find interesting.

Exercise 4: Talk freely with the wall. Do it as if you yourself were, in succession, a very tender child, a decrepit old person, a royal prince or princess, a beggar, and other images that come to mind.

Exercise 5: Repeat Exercises 35, 36, and 37 from Chapter Four.

4. Preparing the Body

Since we are not concerned with the preparation of a professional teller, any one of the many available exercise programs will get your body ready for the exercises in the following section. Nonetheless, I would like to emphasize that for those interested in the subject of this book, the necessary preparation should reflect the idea of "warming up," "becoming aware of," and "loosening up" the joints of the body more than the idea of strengthening the muscles. You should do the following exercises very gently.

Exercise 1: Walk slowly and feel the floor under your feet, being aware of your skeleton and the movement of your muscles and tendons; be particularly conscious of how your joints function.

Exercise 2: Lightly jog. If you don't have the space, jog in place.

Exercise 3: Roll your head gently in a circle, relaxing the neck. Do it very gently and slowly, each time making the circles wider. Let your head fall toward your back when it moves toward the nape of your neck; let it fall toward the chest when the chin moves forward; and point your temples toward the corresponding shoulder when your head moves to the sides. Repeat this movement some ten to fifteen times, first in a clockwise, and then in a counterclockwise direction.

Exercise 4: Gently draw circles in the air with your shoulders. Try to make the circles wider each time.

Exercise 5: Put your elbows against your waist and gently make circles with your forearms, working the elbow joints.

Exercise 6: Stretch your arms out in front of you and make circles in the air with your fists gently closed. Work your wrist joints.

Exercise 7: Keep the same position as in the previous exercise and independently exercise every joint in your hands that you can.

Exercise 8: Gently exercise your spinal column as follows:

a. Try to bring together your forehead (lowering it) and your pelvis (raising it). Then assume the opposite position: lowering the nape and raising the coccyx. Repeat several times.
b. Move the left temple (lowering it) and the left hip (raising it) toward each other. Then assume the opposite position: lower the right temple and raise the right hip. Repeat several times.

Exercise 9: Make circles in the air with your hips, as if you were moving a hula hoop.

Exercise 10: Put all the weight of your body on your right leg and gently balance the left leg. This exercise will loosen the upper femoral joint. Put the weight of your body on the left leg and gently balance the right leg.

Exercise 11: Put all the weight of your body on your right leg and lift your left knee to approximately the height of your hip. In that position make circles in the air with the left ankle, working the knee joint. Now put the weight of your body on your left leg and do the same exercise with the right knee.

Exercise 12: Put all the weight of your body on your right leg and slightly lift your left foot. Make circles in the air with the tip of your foot, exercising the ankle joint. Now put the weight of your body on your left leg and repeat the exercise with the right ankle.

Exercise 13: Alternately contract and expand all the muscles of your face.

5. Developing Body Expression

You should do the physical conditioning exercises before carrying out the following series:

Exercise 1: Experiment with various manners of walking, beginning with these situations: hurried, distracted, tired, sad, happy, apathetic, bewildered, fleeing, and pursued. Go from one manner to another freely, without worrying about following the order in which they are listed here.

Exercise 2: Experiment with various manners of walking, imagining that you are walking on: thorns, eggs, sand, water, thick oatmeal porridge, and mercury. Come up with your own images.

Exercise 3: Experiment with various manners of walking. Imagine that you are each of the following: a child, an old person, a cripple, a robot, a marching soldier, a dog, a cat, a rat, an elephant, a bird, and a monkey.

Each of these "characters" could experiment with various emotional states. Think up your own images.

Exercise 4: Experiment with various ways of performing the following activities, using various imaginary objects: picking up, handing over, placing, throwing, taking, folding, touching, shaking and shaping. Go from one type of action to another freely, without worrying about following the order given here. Come up with your own ideas.

Exercise 5: Experiment with various ways of doing the following: stretching, drawing up, bending, twisting, floating, sitting down (without using any real support), falling, getting up, shaking, and hurling. Come up with your own ideas.

Exercise 6: Experiment with various ways of physically responding to the stimulus of imaginary winds: breezes, soft winds, stronger winds, hurricanes, and whirlwinds. Each one could vary and be, for example, cold, hot, of continual or variable intensity and direction, humid, dry, or aromatic. Think up your own ideas.

Exercise 7: Experiment with various forms of dance, preferably in accompaniment to rhythms and melodies that appeal to you but that you have never danced to before. Consider such music as classical pieces, sacred music, lullabies, the tango, the samba, military marches, advertising jingles, or the Happy Birthday song. Come with your own ideas.

Exercise 8: Stand facing a bare wall and experiment with various exaggerated facial expressions—perhaps I should say "funny faces"—with the following objectives in mind: frightening, moving, seducing, and surprising someone; making someone laugh; and making someone cry. Think up your own ideas.

Exercise 9: Repeat Exercises 34, 35, 36 and 37 from Chapter Four.

PART TWO

STORYTELLING APPLICATIONS IN THE HOME AND SOCIAL LIFE AND IN EDUCATIONAL, SOCIAL AND CULTURAL PROGRAMS

How to Tell Stories: A Latin American Perspective

In various times and cultures, human beings have turned to storytelling to be entertained or to find delight in the beauty of words. Storytelling has also had many social functions, among them the following: to provide information about health and nutrition, handling tools and instruments, and executing technical processes; to preserve and disseminate beliefs, heroic deeds, and histories of families, clans, and peoples; and to disseminate knowledge and provide a catharsis for sailors, hunters, miners and others who perform dangerous work. Storytelling continues to have several of these functions in modern cities, and other functions have been added that are directly related to the dynamics of urban life and its institutions. Indeed, storytellers have accomplished a great deal in the application of their art in many different social settings.

Fields for Applying the Art of Storytelling

You can tell stories for pure pleasure, of course. That is the basic, fundamental reason for storytelling. Let us hope that whoever tells a story does it, above all, for pleasure. If people don't derive pleasure from telling, it is better that they not do it at all, and if they find themselves obligated to tell stories for work-related reasons, I believe that they have only two alternatives: either look for another job or else succeed in finding pleasure in storytelling. In any event, there are many different and very interesting ways to apply storytelling in the home, in social life, in education and in different types of social and cultural programs.

In Part Two, you will find some options for storytelling applications as well as some activities and proposals for putting them into practice. I have already had success with most of these activities, and though I haven't personally tried some of them, the similar experiments I have done and the results of psychological, social, and educational research I have studied lead me to believe that they can be applied with equal success. Many of the activities can be done for a variety of purposes in various social settings. Perhaps what is most important for you, for me, and for the art that unites us is that you take these comments solely as a point of departure or inspiration for developing your own ideas about areas for application and that you successfully create proposals and specific activities for them.

There are many objectives for the application of storytelling, and they vary according to the social setting.

In the home, storytelling strengthens ties, cultivates and enriches the family's oral tradition, entertains the family, and introduces topics for conversation. It helps children learn to listen attentively, develop concentration skills, improve their memory, increase verbal comprehension, develop their verbal, facial, and body expression, enrich their vocabulary, develop their aesthetic sensitivity and imagination, expand their referential world, and confront adverse circumstances.

In the school, in addition to serving the purposes stated above, storytelling can increase opportunities for communication, enhance the enjoyment of reading, and stimulate creative expression in music and in the plastic and dramatic arts.

In the home, the school, the literary workshop or any other setting, storytelling leads to an intense and enthusiastic awareness of language, and it sensitizes one to the beauty of words and the value of silences. In general, it reveals the pleasure that a verbal composition can bring.

In both the elementary school and in the education of youth and adults, storytelling serves to introduce academic topics in a pleasant way.

In the library, as in the home or the school, it is an excellent resource for encouraging reading.

In museums, tourist attractions, and historical or archeological sites, it is an entertaining way to disseminate necessary information.

Good tellers of anecdotes, jokes and stories are appreciated at social gatherings for their ability to delight their listeners.

With groups of small children and in camps or vacationing groups of juveniles, storytelling serves to entertain, to suggest potentially constructive situations, to encourage reflection, and to promote the exchange of ideas.

In psychotherapy classes, it can serve to stimulate the projections of the unconscious and the resolution of conflicts.

In the business world, good lecturers and speakers turn to the art of storytelling, relating jokes and anecdotes to liven up their speeches or presentations.

Storytelling is an effective tool for developing programs to disseminate literature and promote the enjoyable reading of literary works.

It serves to create an opportunity for meeting and getting to know others and for exchanging information, opinions, and knowledge within a community.

It can also be applied in social and cultural programs for a range of purposes:

- communication
- literacy
- popular education
- rural education
- health education
- nutrition education

- education about the environment
- introducing new technologies
- revitalizing and utilizing traditional lore
- revitalizing dying languages
- encouraging self-esteem and strengthening the cultural identity of ethnic minorities in migratory situations or in the process of ethnic development
- entertainment and therapeutic aims in work with social groups in crisis situations, such as street children
- providing entertainment and support in orphanages, homes for the elderly, and hospitals.

In general, storytelling facilitates group cohesion and identification in every situation. It can also be an invaluable instrument for stimulating mutual awareness of knowledge and dreams. Remember that our dreams expand when we share them.

At any rate, it is not a question of choosing between telling for the sake of telling or telling for the purpose of application. On some occasions, you may tell simply because it gives you pleasure and, on others, to satisfy specific expectations and needs. In fact, when you are a teller, people often come up to you with requests and specific concerns. You should not be closed to the idea in advance. If you take their requests and concerns into account, you can derive pleasure from being useful, and you can discover new possibilities for your expressive and creative development. Just imagine the possibility of telling for the blind or the possibility of promoting education or community development with your storytelling. Imagine creating these kinds of possibilities or putting them into practice for the human pleasure of giving and for the no less human pleasure of growing as a creative individual!

Storytelling Activities and Applications

We need to remember that merely by telling a story we stimulate our audience; regardless of our intentions, we affect our listeners' sensitivity, emotional state, imagination, memory, and reasoning. Perhaps you have already experienced a spontaneous reaction on the part of your listeners and have understood that you must give them time to respond to what has touched them. But it is also possible to produce this effect on purpose. So why not take the initiative and propose doing something that will pique their interest?

In the following pages, you will find thirty proposals, each of them consisting of an activity and a list of its applications. Several variants may be included with the proposals. In all, more than sixty variants are given, and when they are added to the thirty activities, the result is more than ninety different proposals. Not all of the activities can be applied to all audiences: some of them are appropriate only for children, others only for adults. You know your audience best, and you can best decide whether you should or shouldn't do a certain activity or whether or not modifying an activity would be something you would want to pursue.

I suggest that you read through the activities and their applications. As you read them one by one, you can decide which ones are of interest to you and fall within your abilities, which ones do not, at least for now, and which ones you might want to investigate further. Whatever the case, you will associate them with your own experiences, and probably others will occur to you: give them thought and try them out. I hope you enjoy the adventure!

Activity 1. After telling one or more stories, ask your listeners how they imagine some of the characters. Be patient, and don't speak before you need to. Encourage the audience with your facial expression and ask additional questions that refer to the actions of the characters; make it clear that you truly want to be given many descriptions. As you will see, they will begin to appear. Let the first person (adult, youth, or child) speak for as long as he wants and keep the audience interested in his participation. If no one wants to speak, question the group as a whole, or question some member who seems to want to participate but is too shy to do so. Continue doing this as long as it seems appropriate, given the interest of the group. Then you can move on to another activity or reward your audience with a new story.

Applications. This activity can help in the following ways: to stimulate the listeners' imagination and verbal expression; to conquer stage fright or fear of speaking in public; to "break the ice" and facilitate group cohesion; to illustrate for educational or therapeutic purposes the "word-imagination-word" relationship; to show for educational or therapeutic purposes the "word-evocation of experiences-construction of images" relationship; and to serve as the first step in using some of the activities given below. This activity can also be used to stimulate reading if there is information about where to find the stories, other stories like them, or relevant books and if participants are not made to feel obligated to read them.

Activity 2. After telling one or more stories, ask those present to draw the scenes or the characters that they liked best. You will have to insist that it doesn't matter whether they know how to draw. You will be amazed at the results. Of course, to challenge your audience's imagination, it would be best for you to choose stories that include such stimuli as colors, characters with unusual physical traits, or solely imaginary characters with no evident relationship to real people.

Applications. This activity can promote the expression of the visual arts and the development of various intellectual skills, demonstrating for educational or therapeutic purposes the "word-image-graphics" relationship. It can also serve to stimulate reading if information is provided about where to find your stories, other stories like them, or relevant books and if participants are not made to feel that they have to read them.

Activity 3. After telling one or more stories, invite those present to act out how the characters walk, eat, or perform any other action.

Applications. The activity will add enthusiasm to social gatherings of children, youths, or those adults capable of playful fun. In a classroom or other setting, this activity could also help participants develop their acting ability and express themselves through body movement; promote the development of intellectual skills; "break the ice" and facilitate the integration of the members of a group; and put a stop to an undesirable situation. As with previous activities, this one can serve to stimulate reading if there is information about where to find the stories, others like them, or relevant books and if participants are not required to read them.

Activity 4 (especially for small children). After telling a story, ask those present who performed this or that action in the story. Also ask them to describe characters and episodes.

Applications. This activity develops intellectual skills and verbal expression.

Activity 5 (especially for children). After telling a story, ask the listeners to name—orally or in writing—the human beings, the other living beings, and the objects in the story in the order of their appearance.

Applications. This activity helps to develop intellectual skills and verbal expression (oral or written, or both, according to how it is applied). It can also serve to stimulate reading if there is information about where to find the stories, others like them, or relevant books and if the children are not made to feel that they must read them.

Activity 6 (especially for children): After telling a story, ask the children to retell it in their own words—orally, in writing, or both.

Applications. The same as for Activity 5.

Activity 7 (especially for school). After telling a story, ask the children to illustrate their favorite scenes, take the illustrations to their homes, and retell the story while showing their pictures to their families. Explain to them that they are free to re-create the story without worrying about the details. The next day in class the children will recount their experience.

Applications. This activity can serve to develop intellectual skills and verbal and artistic expression, and it can also stimulate parent-child and home-school relationships.

Activity 8 (especially for children). After telling a story, ask each child to illustrate his or her favorite scene. Then, with everyone's participation and under your guidance, have the children put the drawings into chronological order.

Applications. The activity develops intellectual skills and verbal and artistic expression; it also promotes group cohesion and the ability to state and debate opinions. As always, the activity can serve to stimulate reading provided that there is information about where to find the stories, others like them, or relevant books and that the children are not made to feel that reading them is required.

Activity 9. After telling a story, ask those present to transform it into a cartoon or "comic strip."

Variants. There are various developmental alternatives with this activity since the children can do it all together, in small groups, or individually.

Applications. The activity will serve to develop intellectual skills and enhance artistic, verbal, and written expression. Depending on the variant adopted, it can also stimulate group integration. This activity will make the listeners more inclined to read if they are informed as to where they can find the story, stories like it, or relevant books and if they aren't made to feel obligated to read them.

Activity 10. After telling two or more stories, ask those present to analyze and compare the apparel, food, costumes, and type of housing found in the different stories or to compare the features found in one story with the circumstances in their own lives.

Applications. This activity stimulates intellectual skills, and, depending on the stories chosen, allows the listeners to make comparisons in culture, history, society, and geography. It could also be used to start a class on one of these subjects.

Activity 11. After telling various stories, ask those present to change the ending.

Variants. They can do it all together, in small groups, or individually and in written or oral form.

Applications. This activity can serve to add enthusiasm to a group game, to develop intellectual skills, and to promote verbal expression and creativity—oral or written, as the case may be. It can also be used to stimulate group cohesion.

Activity 12 ("Transforming Stories"). After telling a story, work with the audience to establish the sequence of the principal actions (we learned this procedure in Chapter Three). Introduce a change in the main character, the primary situation, the setting, or the social context of the story and then ask the audience to re-create the story, incorporating the changes.

Variants. As with the previous activity, there are several variants. It can be done individually or in groups, and it can be done orally, in writing, as a cartoon, as mime, or in dramatic form.

Applications. This activity is useful for encouraging group play, for stimulating group integration, and for guiding group members to express, exchange, and discuss opinions about how to resolve problematic situations. You could suggest the situations when proposing the modification mentioned above or you could ask the group to do it. This activity can also be used to initiate situations for psychodrama.

Activity 13 ("Creating Origins"). After telling stories of origin or transformation, point out to your audience the specific way in which they explain how human beings, animals, plants or other natural phenomena first appeared with the features that characterize them today. Then suggest that your audience invent the origin of other interesting phenomena such as how the sea began to have waves, how butterfly wings began to have colors, or how lionesses lost their manes.

Variants. The stories can be created with everyone working together under your guidance, in small groups, or individually. These three variants can also be done in succession. Finally, ask for their stories in writing.

Applications. This activity will serve to encourage group play, develop new intellectual skills, and enhance verbal expression and creativity—either oral or written, as the case may be. It can also stimulate group cohesion and initiate situations for psychodrama.

Activity 14. After telling several stories, ask those present to create their own stories, beginning with a phrase that you provide them.

Applications. This activity can serve to promote group play, develop intellectual skills, and facilitate oral or written verbal expression. It can stimulate group cohesion. It can also encourage group members to express and discuss opinions; the discussion can involve subjects from "real life," depending on the beginning phrase you provide them. It can encourage reading if there is information about where to find the stories, other stories like them, or relevant books and if participants aren't made to feel that the reading is obligatory.

Activity 15. After telling various stories, ask those present to create one that includes a well-known, popular refrain.

Variants. You can offer the same refrain to everyone, or each participant can choose his own. In addition, the group can work individually or in subgroups, orally or in writing, or in both modes in turn.

Applications. This activity can serve to develop intellectual skills and promote both oral and written forms of verbal expression and creation. It can encourage group play and stimulate group integration. It is also useful for encouraging group members to express and discuss opinions; the discussion can include "real life" subjects, depending on the beginning phrase that you choose. This activity can be used in psychotherapy as well.

Activity 16. After telling a story, ask those present to invent a dance.

Variants. Instead of a dance, you can ask that they create a song, a poem, background music, or a poster that announces your telling of the story. They can work all together in a group, in small groups, or individually.

Applications. This exercise can encourage group play, improve intellectual skills, and promote verbal, musical, and artistic expression as well as expression through body movement and dance. It can also foster group integration and encourage group members to state and discuss their opinions.

Activity 17. After telling a story, ask those present to perform a theatrical adaptation of it.

Variants. This activity can be done by the group as a whole or in small groups. Depending on the make-up of the group and the availability of time and resources, there can be varying degrees of complexity and technical perfection in the play and the participants' execution of it. The participants can be guided to undertake specialized tasks such as adaptation, direction, performance, costumes, and stage scenery.

Applications. This activity can serve to develop intellectual skills, verbal and artistic expression, and experience with stage production. It can also foster group integration and encourage the participants to express and discuss their opinions.

Activity 18. After telling at least two stories, ask for a summary of both of them.

Variants. The summary can be done by the group as a whole, in small groups, or individually. It can be done orally, in writing, as dramatization, or as a cartoon.

Applications. This activity can encourage group play, develop intellectual abilities, enhance oral and written skills, and encourage expression through art or drama, as the case may be. It can foster group integration, as well as the statement and discussion of opinions among group members. It can also promote reading if it provides information about where to find the stories told, ones that are similar, or relevant books.

Activity 19. After telling a story, ask those present to re-create it from the point of view of one of the characters.

Variants. Read the variants for Activity 18.

Applications. This activity can encourage group play, develop intellectual abilities, enhance both speaking and writing skills, and encourage expression through art or drama. It can also foster the integration of group members and encourage them to express and discuss their opinions.

Activity 20. After telling a story, you can encourage an evaluation process with such questions as who the most important character is and why; how one or another event could have been avoided; and what relation the story has to an event with which the participants are intimately connected.

Application. This exercise can help alleviate stage fright, promote group integration, and encourage group members to state and discuss their opinions.

Activity 21. After telling several stories, analyze any one of them, clearly identifying the protagonist and the antagonist. Next, ask the participants to choose any one of the other stories you told and to write down on three small pieces of paper what, in their opinion, the name or identity of the protagonist is, what the name or identity of the antagonist is, and where the events took place. Then put the three separate groups of papers into three containers—hats, bags, or boxes, for example. The participants take a paper from each of the containers, and on the basis of the three that they have drawn, they create a new story and tell it to the group.

Variants. Once the example has been made with one of the stories you told, you can tell the participants to write down the names of the main characters and the relevant places from any story that they remember. Depending on how many people are in the group and on what their interests are, you can also request that they write down their new story.

Applications. The results of this exercise are similar to those of Exercise 18.

Activity 22. After telling some stories chosen from the history of your family, ask your listeners to draw on their memories and tell stories from their own family history.

Variants. Instead of telling stories from your family history to community or social groups, you can tell stories about such subjects as local history, customs, immigration and labor experiences, and you can then encourage your listeners to share stories on similar topics.

Applications. This activity can be applied in the school or in settings of social development. Depending on the variant selected and the context of the application, you can orient the activity to accomplish such goals as developing intellectual skills in general; initiating social research; developing oral and written expression; stimulating family and intergenerational communication; learning to value one's own past; becoming familiar with such experiences as immigration and labor situations; and stimulating the development of local oral history.

Activity 23. After telling several carefully selected stories, ask those present if they find any relation between these stories and their own life experience. If you ask a question like this, the group should of course be relatively small, and group members should have some degree of confidence in you and in each other. Wait, give them time, repeat the question in various ways, and encourage them with questions of a complementary nature. Wait; be patient.

Applications. This exercise can be useful for improving communication in a group, particularly for guiding communication to subjects that the group members do not usually explore. It encourages the statement and discussion of opinions. It also serves to stimulate enjoyment of verbal compositions, and it facilitates the development of various intellectual skills. It can be used in psychotherapy as well.

Activity 24 ("Exquisite Corpse," adaptation of a game played by the surrealists). After telling several stories that stimulate your listeners' imagination, ask them to be seated in a circle. Explain the rules that are detailed below and begin the game yourself. You will start telling a story that you make up as you go along. Tell it spontaneously and automatically, without stopping to think about your content and not even choosing your words. After a moment, either when it seems appropriate to you given what you have already told or after a previously determined period of time, tap your neighbor on the shoulder. He should continue the story immediately, without losing the rhythm and telling the story in the same automatic way that you did. All those present will participate in the same fashion until the round is finished. If you wish, everyone can participate in successive rounds in the same

Storytelling Applications in the Home and Social Life

order as in the first. The last player will create an ending to the story. Before beginning the game, you should limit how long each person can speak (one minute, for example).

Variants. Other rules can be introduced such as: each player's participation lasts as long as another player keeps a top or bottle spinning; before adding his own contribution, a player must repeat what the player before him said; the voices of the characters introduced by each player must be imitated; when the game is finished, all the players write down the story as they remember it and then the versions are compared.

Applications. This activity will add enthusiasm to social gatherings of children, youths, or adults capable of playful fun. It could also be done in a classroom or in any other setting to stimulate the work of the imagination and to encourage verbal expressiveness, either oral or written, depending on the variant adopted. In addition, it can be used to further the development of intellectual skills, to "break the ice," and to facilitate the cohesion of members of a group. It is an extremely valuable training exercise for developing a beginning teller's ability to improvise, and its usefulness in training workshops is highly recommended.

Activity 25 ("Tall Tales Championship"). After telling one or more tall tales, invite those present to participate in this championship. Each player, in turn, will tell one or more of the most absurd and ridiculous tales possible but with an air of absolute sincerity. Of course, it is only a game, and all the players will adopt an attitude of naive trust in the teller whose turn it is. Each teller must do his best to make his lie more absurd or exaggerated that the one before and at the same time act as though he believes that what he is saying is true.

Variants. A topic can be decided upon before the game begins, or each player can choose his own topic. The winner can be chosen by secret ballot or by open deliberation and voice vote.

Applications. This activity can serve to enliven social gatherings of children, youths, or adults capable of playful fun. It can also be done in a classroom, or in any other setting, to stimulate the play of imagination and oral verbal expressiveness, to promote the development of intellectual skills, to "break the ice," and to facilitate group cohesion. It can promote the statement and discussion of opinions. In addition, it is extremely valuable for training a beginning teller's ability to fabricate, and its use in workshops for beginners is highly recommended. It can encourage reading if information is given about where to find the same stories, similar tales, or relevant books and if participants are not made to feel obligated to read them.

Activity 26 ("Batting Practice"). After telling some stories to create a pleasant atmosphere and stimulate the participants' imagination, you can suggest having "batting practice." The players form a circle and one of them, who will be the "batter," is in the center. One by one, those in the circle "pitch" beginnings of stories (tales, tall tales, anecdotes, or histories, for example). There won't be pre-established turns for pitching, so each player will be able to pitch at any time, but the players forming the circle must be careful to let only one person speak at a time. The batter responds by immediately looking at and directing his attention to the pitcher who is throwing (that is, speaking). As soon as the pitcher finishes, the batter, without losing an instant, develops the story by introducing a new situation. It isn't necessary for the batter to bring the story to a conclusion. How long each batter should "play" will be stipulated beforehand. One by one, all the players take the batter's place. You can be the "umpire" (that is, the coordinator), or you can participate in the game as a player.

Variants. A topic can be decided upon before the beginning of the game, or there can be complete freedom with respect to choice of topic. The winner can be chosen by secret ballot or by group deliberation and voice vote. When the game is over, you can also ask those present to develop in writing the story that interested them most.

Applications. This activity can heighten enthusiasm in social gatherings of children, youths, or adults capable of playful fun. In a school classroom, or in any other setting, it could serve the same purpose, or it could be used to stimulate the participants' imagination as well as their oral or written expressiveness, depending on the variant adopted. It can serve to "break the ice," facilitate integration among members of a group, and guide the group to express and discuss their opinions. This activity is valuable for training a beginning teller's ability to improvise, and it is highly recommended in workshops for beginners. It can encourage reading if it gives information about where to find the stories, similar ones, or relevant books and if participants are not made to feel obligated to read them.

Activity 27 ("Tell it through mime"). Divide those present into two or more groups. Meet in a separate area with representatives of each group and tell them a story. The representatives then tell the story to their respective groups only through mime, without using any words at all. Each group has an agreed upon an amount of time to deliberate in private and try to reconstruct the story. After deliberating, the group develops a written version of the story that was originally told through mime. Finally, all of the participants are brought together, and each group reads its version of the story.

Applications. This exercise can serve to liven up social gatherings of children, youths, or adults capable of playful fun. It can be done in a classroom or in any other setting to stimulate the participants' imagination and to enhance their ability to express themselves verbally and with body movement. It facilitates the cohesion of group members by "breaking the ice," and it fosters the development of intellectual skills. It encourages participants to express and discuss their opinions. In addition, it is extremely useful for developing the ability for mimicry, and it is highly recommended in workshops for beginning tellers.

Activity 28. After telling two or three stories by the same author, give the author's name and the title of the book or books where you found the stories. Don't make reading the stories obligatory; don't even request that your listeners read them. Let the reading be voluntary.

Applications. This activity can be used to promote reading in schools and libraries.

Activity 29. Tell two or three stories of the same type (adventure, romance, fantasy, or science fiction, for example). Provide the authors' names and the titles of books where the stories can be found and mention that the books contain more stories as well. Don't make the reading obligatory or even ask your listeners to read the stories. Let them do it voluntarily.

Applications. This activity can be used to promote reading in schools and libraries.

Activity 30 ("Unfinished Story"). After telling several stories, share the beginning of another that promises to be more interesting than the ones before and then stop telling. Before the almost certain demand from an audience of children or youths that you finish the story, provide the name of the book where they can find the story and read it in its entirety, or you can have copies of the story on hand for those who request it. Don't make the reading obligatory or even request that your listeners read the stories. Let them do it voluntarily.

Applications. This exercise can be used to promote reading in schools and libraries.

PART THREE

STORIES READY TO TELL

Part Three of the book offers four stories that are ready to tell. For each of them I give first the text and then the column of "Principal Actions," as in the outline we learned to prepare in Chapter Three. I also make some suggestions about how the story could be told. The column of "Dialogues and/or Complementary Details" is deliberately left blank so that you can decide what seems appropriate to you and construct the dialogues yourself.

How to Tell Stories: A Latin American Perspective

The Mucurutú

by Daniel Mato

Long, long ago, when the world was still being formed and the sky was not yet full of stars, a strange tree appeared in the forests. It can be seen today in Venezuela in the mountains surrounding the beaches of Choroní, on the Caribbean Sea.

It was a strong and beautiful tree whose flowers and fruit did not grow from its long branches but rather hung from its trunk. Its fruit were immense spheres, clustered together and so perfectly regular and identical that they seemed manmade. And the flowers did not look like flowers but like open mouths: the petals were red, and, in the center, a crown of very white teeth was adorned with a yellow halo.

The tree was the only one of its kind. There was no other like it, and soon it attracted the interest of the animals on the mountain, not only because of its majestic and exotic beauty but also because a penetrating, delicious fragrance wafted from its flowers and spread throughout the air. It attracted huge clouds of hummingbirds that hovered in the air like miniature helicopters and sucked from the flowers with their long beaks; it drew multitudes of bees, and intrepid spiders spun their sparkling nets among the branches of the tree to catch all the insects.

In short time, the tree became a hectic, crowded scene of birds and insects, and soon they began to hear the tree wailing, "Mucurutú, Mucurutú … ." The tree's bitter lament resounded throughout the forest; in spite of so much company, it felt alone, for there was no other tree like it in the world.

"Mucurutú, Mucurutú … ." the jay birds appeared to call mockingly from the tops of near-by trees, accompanied by choruses of troupials and thrushes.

"Mucurutú, Mucurutú …," the tree seemed to echo, adding to its solitude the sadness of not even having a name.

A young Carib Indian who was walking by suddenly stopped, amazed to see such a boisterous celebration of birds and flowers. The echoing lament of the tree filled the youth's ears and so greatly affected him that from deep within his being rose the cry "Mucurutú!" He immediately ran to his village to tell his people that there was a new tree on the mountain.

The tree remained behind in the forest, alone and nameless, astonished at having seen a human being and having heard a human voice for the first time.

The Carib Indian arrived at his village breathless from running and visibly moved. Everyone immediately gathered round to hear his story.

"It's an immense tree, and its round fruit hangs in clusters, and its flowers look like beautiful mouths. But the tree is sad, and it's crying."

"Are you sure it's crying?" asked his astonished father.

"Yes, Father, it's crying; you can hear it moan, 'mucurutú, mucurutú', as if its heart of wood were breaking."

"The tree must feel very lonely," said the eldest in the village. "That's what happens to all animals, trees and bushes that live their lives without seeing another of their kind close by."

"Yes, we have to hurry and give it a name: that will calm the tree and at least let it know that we understand it and appreciate its visiting our forest. That's what our ancestors did every time a new being came to these mountains," added another elder.

"Call it 'Mucurutú,'" suggested the youth who had found the tree and had been so deeply moved at hearing its lament.

"Mucurutú, Mucurutú," repeated all the Indians gathered there.

"Agreed, Mucurutú will be its name," said the eldest. And they all left to give the tree its name.

As the Indians drew near the site of the forest where that splendid tree was, they could hear, ever more clearly, its lament and the commotion of the birds around it. All the forest seemed to resound with a song of welcome to the new tree.

After finding the impetuous, crystalline river that flowed down from the highest point of the mountain, they walked along its bank to a cascade of stones. Then they climbed up the stones to the top. When they reached the top, there where the forest was a little more open, they suddenly came upon a wondrous sight: the immense canopy of green leaves, the colorful mouths, the huge fruit and the frenzied activity of the birds. Everything was sparkling in the sun.

Overcome by the lament of the majestic tree, the amazed natives contemplated the scene in silence for a long time. Then suddenly, as though obeying an inner impulse, they all rushed toward it exclaiming, "Mucurutú, Mucurutú, Mucurutú!"

The tree immediately understood that these people had just given it a name, and it was so excited that it let some of its fruit fall.

The huge spheres were heavy and plump, filled with seeds, and they crashed to the ground. Then the squirrels and the peccaries ran over to see what was happening, and they immediately began to eat the tree's seeds and the delicious flesh of its fruit.

The Indians lost no time in catching a pair of the peccaries, and they returned to the village with provisions for their people. Meanwhile, the rest of the peccaries and the squirrels quickly fled to other parts of the mountain. When the seeds passed through their digestive system and were expelled, the animals, without even knowing it, began to sow new Mucurutús everywhere.

So, with time, the tree not only had a name, but it also began to feel that it was no longer alone. Ever since then, Mucurutú trees have grown in the mountains of the Choroní coasts and in humid and warm forests farther inland, in the green lands of the Americas. *[Author's Note]*

Outline for Telling the Story

Introduction: Long, long ago, when the world was still being formed and the sky was not yet full of stars, there appeared in the forests a strange tree that can be seen today in the mountains surrounding the beaches of Choroní, on the Caribbean Sea. It was a strong and beautiful tree whose flowers and fruit did not grow from its long branches but rather hung from its trunk. Its fruit were immense spheres, clustered together and so perfectly regular and identical that they seemed manmade. And the flowers did not look like flowers but like open mouths: their petals were red, and, in the center, a crown of very white teeth was adorned with a yellow halo. But the beautiful tree was sad because there was no other tree like it, and it didn't even have a name.

Principal Actions	Dialogues and/or Complementary Details
1. It was the only tree of its kind, and it soon attracted the interest of all the animals on the mountain.	
2. In short time the tree became a busy, crowded scene of birds and insects that began to hear its lament: [Mucurutú, Mucurutú …]	
3. The tree's bitter lament resounded throughout the forest.	
4. Jay birds, troupials and thrushes mocked it: [Mucurutú, Mucurutú …]	
5. The tree responded to this mockery by repeating its lament: [Mucurutú, Mucurutú …]	

Principal Actions	**Dialogues and/or Complementary Details**
6. A young Carib Indian was passing by, and he stopped to contemplate that celebration of birds and flowers.	
7. The tree's lament and its echo filled the youth's ears and moved him to such an extent that from deep within him rose a cry: [Mucurutú!]	
8. The young Indian ran to his village to tell his people that there was a new tree on the mountain.	
9. When he arrived at the village, everyone gathered around to hear what he had to say.	
10. Since they thought that the tree's lament was the result of the its feeling alone and being nameless, they decided to go comfort it by giving it a name, as was their custom in these situations. The young Indian proposed calling it "Mucurutú," and everyone agreed.	
11. They all left together to give the tree a name.	
12. The closer they got to the site in the forest where the tree was, the more clearly they heard its lament and the commotion of the birds around it: the entire forest was ringing with sound.	
13. The natives fell silent, contemplating the tree and overcome by its lament.	
14. After a long time, everyone suddenly felt compelled to run to the tree at the same time, exclaiming, " Mucurutú, Mucurutú, Mucurutú!"	

Principal Actions	Dialogues and/or Complementary Details
15. The tree understood that these people had just given it a name, and it was so excited that it carelessly let some of its fruit drop.	
16. The squirrels and the peccaries hurried to eat the fruit, which was full of seeds, and then they fled to other areas in the mountain.	

Ending: In this way, the squirrels and the peccaries, by ingesting and expelling the seeds, unknowingly began to sow new Mucurutús everywhere. Thus, with time, the tree not only had a name but also began to sense that it had companions.

Ever since that time, Mucurutús have grown in the mountains of the Choroní coasts and farther inland, in the green lands of the Americas.

Ideas for Telling the Story

It would be best, of course, for you to familiarize yourself with the tree in question by examining either the tree itself or pictures of it. But if that isn't possible, don't be disappointed. The description included in the story, your knowledge of other trees, and your imagination will come to your aid.

How do you imagine the Mucurutú? Try using your body to represent the trunk, the branches, the tree's attitude before and after having a name, and the tree while it is lamenting and while hearing the mocking reply of the birds. These are scenes from the story that you could depict.

Don't miss the opportunity to cry "Mucurutú, Mucurutú" as many times as it occurs in the story. That is why I marked this phrase in brackets in the "Principal Actions" column, so that you wouldn't omit it ... Try it! I imagine it as a bitter and prolonged lament when the tree is solitary. I imagine it happy, unruly and boisterous in the response of the birds. I imagine it deep, unexpected and amazed in the voice of the young Indian when he discovered the tree.

Finally, I imagine it solemn, reverberating and ceremonious when the natives pronounce it in unison. Play with these possibilities. Explore for yourself the expressive possibilities of this lament and the nuances and character of your voice.

And how could you represent the birds in the first scene? Could your hands be, at times, part of the branches and, at times, flying birds? Do you know how to whistle and imitate bird calls? How do birds move their heads? Do they all do it the same way? Of course, it isn't a matter of imitating them but of experiencing them.

How do you imagine the Indian—his emotion, his shout, his race to the village, his story to the rest of the Indians, and his voice? How do you imagine the voice and the demeanor of the elders who speak about the tree's solitude? You could portray the scene of the young Indian's relating his experience while the rest are listening and the scene of the group of Indians as they speak and deliberate about the discovery. Experiment with different voices and demeanors.

How do you imagine the moment in which all the Indians give the tree a name? Make the attempt; shout "Mucurutú" and let your whole body go along with the shout. But shout it in a stirring way—don't forget that you a baptizing a new tree.

How could your arms and hands help you represent the squirrels and peccaries that rush to eat the fruit of the tree and then quickly flee? Could your mouth help you?

I am certain that if you take into account the exercises of Chapters Four, Five, and Six in your search for answers to these questions, you will achieve a moving and vivid telling of the story.

Won, an Old Tibetan Peasant

Free version of a Zen tale by Daniel Mato

Won was a wise, old peasant who lived in the Himalaya Mountains. Perhaps more because he was old than because he was wise, Won had learned to recognize his own limitations and not to wear himself out by struggling against them but rather to find happiness by living in harmony with them.

Once Won went in search of some seeds for his small field. He took the road along narrow gorges, and after a while he noticed that a tiger was following him. Without becoming alarmed, Won began to walk faster, but soon he discovered that there was another tiger, only a few steps ahead, coming cautiously and threateningly toward him.

Won then looked down and could make out at the bottom of the abyss a hundred tigers, waiting for him to fall. He understood immediately that his death was imminent. But when he took a second look, he saw that only a few yards below, stretching out from the side of the mountain, were the trunk and branches of an old cherry tree.

Without hesitating for an instant, Won nimbly threw himself over the edge and wrapped his arms around the trunk of the tree. Although his heart was pounding and he felt dazed, he clung firmly to the old cherry tree. Then he noticed that hanging at the end of one of the branches was an extraordinary cherry. He moved very carefully toward it and stretched out his arm until he could reach it. He took it in his fingers. He contemplated its shape and color with delight. He felt its smooth skin. He reveled in its exquisite aroma. And he brought it to his mouth. He sank his teeth into it just at the moment when the branch broke.

Holding on to the branch, Won fell into the abyss. He didn't fight against the fall since he had learned to recognize his limitations and to find his happiness in harmony with them. Won died, of course. But he died savoring his last cherry.

Outline for Telling the Story

Introduction: Won was a wise, old peasant who lived in the Himalaya Mountains. He had learned to accept his limitations and to find happiness by living in harmony with them.

Principal Actions	Dialogues and/or Complementary Details
1. Won left in search of some seeds for his field.	
2. He took the road along narrow gorges.	
3. He noticed that a tiger was following him, and he walked faster.	
4. He discovered that another tiger was approaching in front of him.	
5. He looked into the abyss and saw a hundred tigers waiting for him to fall.	
6. He discovered an old cherry tree in the side of the mountain.	
7. He threw himself at the cherry tree and wrapped his arms around the trunk.	
8. He discovered a cherry at the end of a branch and moved toward it until he could reach it.	
9. He took it between his fingers, contemplated its shape and color, touched its skin, relished its aroma, and put it in his mouth.	
10. At that moment, the branch broke and Won fell into the abyss.	

Ending: Won did not fight against falling because he had learned to recognize his limitations and to find happiness by being in harmony with them.

Won died, of course. But he died savoring his last cherry.

Ideas for Telling the Story

In a certain sense, this is the simplest of the four stories in this section of the book. It is simple because it is short and has no dialogue. Nonetheless, the philosophy expressed in it demands that it be told with special care.

Cultural differences keep most of us from being familiar with this philosophy. We run the risk of telling the story very badly if we trivialize it by focusing on the simple anecdote and not giving the introduction and ending the significance that they deserve. This story requires of both listener and teller a very special frame of mind. The teller's tone of voice, rhythm, and bearing must convey as much as possible the feeling that this is a very important, meaningful story. I don't believe that you have to make a statement about the significance of a story, or say that a story contains an important teaching or moral, or, still less, impart a moralistic tone to the ending of a story. I don't do any of these things. They seem counterproductive to me, and in a certain sense, anti-aesthetic. I merely believe that when you tell this story, your bearing and your tone should be persuasively eloquent.

If you have information about Zen, it will help you achieve that bearing and tone. If you don't, you have two alternatives. The first is to try to obtain information by consulting a good-quality book written for the general public. The second is to avoid the search for information and put your imagination to use, turning to what you have already learned from movies and television about the importance of wisdom, old age and self-knowledge in these cultures and in the calm solemnity that characterizes them. Add to all these considerations the setting of the story—one of tall, bluish-gray mountains, crowned with clouds and cloaked in mist. You need to create an atmosphere of expectation, telling the story slowly but without letting the pace bore your listeners.

You can use your body and particularly your voice and face to good advantage to tell the story in a sensitive, expressive way. Reflect on the expressive possibilities that the following images convey to you: *you* are walking down a road along a narrow gorge; *you* perceive the existence of the first tiger and then the threatening appearance of the second tiger; and *you* discover the hundred tigers waiting for *you* to fall. You can counterbalance this disturbing emotional line with that of the hope awakened by the discovery of the cherry tree, the decision to leap toward it, the "leap toward hope" itself, and the discovery of the cherry. Finally, by introducing a new emotional line with *your* cautious ascent toward the branch and the ensuing moment of picking the cherry and relishing its qualities, you can create the necessary expectation for delivering the ending of the story. As far as this ending is concerned, it matters little whether you are from the East or from the West; death is always a dramatic and sublime experience. To fall toward it savoring a final cherry cannot be without significance. This significance, and the meaning that you impart to it, must be felt in your voice.

Instead of analyzing these images, give yourself over to the free play of your creative imagination. Remember the exercises that you have learned for stimulating your imagination, body expression, and vocal expression. Play with these elements. Don't forget that that more you dedicate yourself to a story, the more you improve your telling, and the more you explore and develop your expressive and creative abilities, the more you open up new opportunities for personal growth.

The Firefly and the Blackberry Bush

Free version of a traditional Pemon tale by Daniel Mato

The Great Savannah is one of the oldest and most mysterious regions of the Americas. Trees and bushes of every size grow along the rivers that cut through its soft, undulating landscape of gleaming green. Seen from above, the tree-lined rivers look like irregular paths of a more intense green than the rest of the Savannah. The summits of the mountains in this extraordinary landscape are not peaks but rather huge plateaus, and their slopes are formed by massive rocks. Other great stones, some of unusual colors, are bathed by the rivers that cascade over them in waterfalls and cause them to glitter.

The Pemon Indians, descendants of the oldest inhabitants of this amazing region, recount that it was in the Great Savannah that the world was first formed. They also say that at that time, thousands and thousands of years ago, the animals and plants were different from those seen today and, furthermore, they could speak.

In those old times, for example, the fireflies, also called lightning bugs, looked very different from how we know them to be now. They weren't small and blackish in color as they are today. They were large, and their bodies had brilliant red, green, and yellow stripes. Moreover, they didn't have that characteristic little light on their tail that nowadays we see them turning on and off at night.

The blackberry bushes at that time were much larger, almost like trees, and their delicious berries were the size of oranges. Their thorns were much larger and more powerful, almost like the teeth of a jaguar; if an animal or someone walking by unknowingly brushed against them, there was a loud rip: kararai! Therefore, the old Pemons gave the blackberry bushes the name of kararai.

Thousands of years ago in that region, an immense and multicolored firefly once undertook a voyage to a very distant place. He was going to visit some relatives, and in his enthusiasm to see them, he flew and flew and flew, without stopping, until the setting sun caught him by surprise. At that moment the firefly, mateu, as he was called, began to fly in circles at the foot of a hill, looking for a refuge where he could spend the night. A blackberry bush, all dry and bent over, saw the colorful firefly, and she immediately fell in love with him.

Eager to win him over, she offered him food, and, managing with great effort to collect some large drops of dew that could still be found, she gave them to the firefly to drink. Then she accommodated him as best she could with one of her few remaining leaves so that the firefly could use it like a hammock to sleep in. The bush offered him conversation, sang songs to him, and even told him beautiful stories until late into the night. When she believed that she had succeeded in winning the firefly's love, she said:

"Firefly, Firefly, do you want to be my true love?"

The firefly, pretending to be asleep, turned over half way in his hammock-leaf and silently made himself comfortable. The blackberry bush, this time gently stroking his stomach, insisted, "Firefly, Firefly, do you want to be my true love?"

Annoyed, the firefly sat up half way and answered in a gruff voice, "No, Blackberry Bush. I don't feel any attraction to you. You are old and ugly, Kararai, and you don't have any leaves. I could never love you!"

Having said this, the firefly made himself comfortable again and settled down to sleep. The blackberry bush was very sad; she spent the whole night quietly crying. The firefly left very early the next morning when the sun had barely appeared in the sky.

The firefly continued his voyage until he arrived at a beautiful ravine, bathed by a crystalline river flowing swiftly over a bed of large, reddish flagstones streaked with green and yellow. It was the Jasper Ravine. Mateu's relatives lived there in what seemed to be an enchanted forest, right next to that beautiful ravine displaying the same colors as the ancient fireflies. Mateu spent several weeks there in the company of his relatives, drinking dew, telling stories of mystery, and singing to the moon. But finally, he had to return. So as not to lose his way, he returned along the same route he had taken before. And that is how it happened that he unexpectedly encountered the same blackberry bush that had previously given him refuge. But what a surprise! The blackberry bush had greatly changed. She shone with new life, full of leaves and flowers. The firefly couldn't believe it! He had to rub his eyes again and again before he was convinced.

Then he said to her, "Blackberry Bush, how lovely you look. How pretty your leaves and flowers are! You look beautiful, Kararai. Do you want to be my true love?"

"No, Firefly. I don't love you anymore."

"But, Blackberry Bush, lovely Kararai, let me win your affection."

"No, Firefly, say no more about it."

"Then at least tell me, lovely Kararai, what you have done to become so young and beautiful."

"I haven't done anything, Firefly. Some Pemons who were hunting here set me on fire, and it was the fire that rejuvenated me."

"Lovely Kararai, do you think that if I set myself on fire, I'll be rejuvenated and look beautiful like you? And then you'll fall in love with me again?"

"I don't know, Firefly. You can try if you want to. But be careful and don't hurt yourself."

But the firefly didn't hear the blackberry bush's last words because he had seen a flame not far away, and he was already in flight. He beat his wings feverishly in his rush to get to the fire, saying "I want to become young and beautiful like the blackberry bush so she'll love me again!"

He was barely over the flame when he realized that he was being burned, and he beat his wings harder and harder to get away. But the result was to make the flame that was burning his body grow even bigger. The firefly plunged into a puddle of water and put the fire out, but by that time his scorched body had lost its color and was shrunken in size. Moreover, no matter how many times he soaked himself in the water, he never could put out one spark, and it remained forever lit on his tail.

The Pemons say that ever since that time, all fireflies are small and blackish in color and carry a little light on their tail, like the fireflies we know today. The Pemons also say that ever since that time fireflies hover around blackberry bushes in bloom, hoping to win their love.

Outline for Telling the Story

Introduction: The Pemon Indians tell that the world began to be formed there where they live, in the Great Savannah, one of the most beautiful and mysterious regions of the Americas. They say also that at that time the animals and the plants could speak and that they looked different from the way we know them now. For example, the fireflies did not have a little light on their tail and were not small and blackish in color as they are now; instead, they were huge in size, and their bodies had yellow, green, and red stripes. And the blackberry bushes, that the Pemon Indians call *kararai*, were as tall as trees.

How to Tell Stories

Principal Actions	Dialogues and/or Complementary Details
1. A firefly undertook a long voyage to visit some relatives. He flew without stopping until the setting sun caught him by surprise.	
2. He began to fly in circles looking for a place to sleep.	
3. A dry and bent over blackberry bush, kararai, fell in love with him.	
4. The blackberry bush, in order to win him over, offered him food, gave him dew to drink, and found a place for him in one of her few leaves, shaped like a hammock. She also talked with him, sang songs to him and told him stories.	
5. When she believed that the moment was right, she proposed that he be her true love.	
6. The firefly pretended to be asleep.	
7. The bush insisted.	
8. The firefly rejected her rudely and offensively and went to sleep.	
9. The next morning the firefly continued his journey until he came to where his relatives lived.	
10. He spent several weeks with them, until he had to return. So as not to get lost, he followed the same route back.	
11. He suddenly encountered the blackberry bush that he had rejected, but she was rejuvenated, full of leaves and flowers.	
12. The firefly then extolled her beauty and asked her to be his true love, but the blackberry bush rejected him.	

Principal Actions	Dialogues and/or Complementary Details
13. The firefly asked the blackberry bush to at least tell him how she had become so beautiful. The blackberry bush explained that it was the work of a fire.	
14. The firefly decided to throw himself into a fire that he saw nearby with the hope of becoming more attractive and of winning the affection of the blackberry bush.	
15. When he felt that the fire was burning him, he beat his wings to put it out, but he only managed to make the flame more intense.	
16. He threw himself into a puddle of water and was able to put out the fire. But his body had already been scorched and had lost its color and become smaller. In addition, he was left with a spark on his tail that he could not put out.	

Ending: The Pemons say that since that time all fireflies have been small and blackish in color and have carried a little light on their tail, like the fireflies we know today. And ever since then, the Pemons also say, fireflies have hovered around blackberry bushes in bloom, hoping to win their love.

Ideas for Telling the Story

Have you even visited a Pemon community? If not, my first suggestion is that you turn to any work written for the general public and learn about their rich, remarkable culture.

Have you visited the Great Savannah? Do you at least know it through photographs or the stories of friends? If you answer "no" to these questions, you would find it helpful to familiarize yourself with that unusual landscape through photographs in an encyclopedia or a book about the region. Otherwise, you have two paths: try to imagine the landscape based on the description from the story; or adapt the story and set it in a landscape that you actually know and find appealing.

I also advise you to learn about blackberry bushes and fireflies if you don't already know them from direct experience. Even if you have seen the sparkle of fireflies at night, you will find it beneficial to consult an illustration and learn more about their anatomical characteristics.

How do fireflies fly?

How long has it been since you flew? Come on; remember that as a child you imitated airplanes when you played with your siblings and friends. Perhaps you have done this even more recently, while playing with your children or nieces and nephews.

In any case, stand up, close the door of the room, and fly. Come on; stretch out your arms on both sides of your body and move through space. Aha! Very good. Now beat your wings. Aha! Remember, this time you aren't an airplane, you are a firefly. Play, experiment, enjoy. Feel like a firefly; get tired of flying so that when you reach the blackberry bush you will feel what the firefly from the story felt. As soon as you have the chance, repeat this experiment outside. Don't be afraid of looking ridiculous, or you will get sick from being too serious! If you still have misgivings, take a child from your family out for a walk and play at flying with him. Later, when you are telling about the flight of the firefly, resurrect these experiences or at least the memory of the more distant ones, when you were a child and dared to fly. Resurrecting the experiences or memories doesn't necessarily mean that you will flap your arms each time you talk about the flight of the firefly. No, not at all. It simply means that when you tell about the flight, you will let these images help you, perhaps lead you to illustrate it in an abbreviated way, with the movement of one hand or one arm or possibly with the movement of your eyes alone. Perhaps at some point you will find it appealing to fly, or at least to extend your arms as if they were the firefly's wings while you present some of his dialogues with the blackberry bush. Incidentally, what will the firefly's voice be like when he's half asleep? And when he is dazzled by the beauty of the blackberry bush whose love he had scorned before?

While on the subject of the dialogues, what will the blackberry bush's voice and manner of speaking be like when she is trying to make the firefly fall in love with her? And how will that same, indifferent blackberry bush speak some weeks later? What will her body be like? Familiarize yourself with a real bush, and if that isn't possible, find some illustrations in an encyclopedia or specialized work. How could you use your body to help your audience imagine what a bush that is unfamiliar to them looks like? It isn't a question of offering an exact representation of the bush; not only is an exact representation impossible, but it wouldn't be very interesting. Think, however, about the particular characteristics that this bush has. Are its branches long? Is it fairly flexible? What kind of contour does it display? Play a little with imitating it. What happens? What do you feel? Can you sense the leaves and the fruit growing from your arms? How will a blackberry bush in love feel? Again, the purpose of this exploration is not to determine voices, gestures or movements to use when you tell the story but simply to generate, explore and develop your own images of what occurs in the story. If you pursue these suggestions conscientiously and with enjoyment and if you turn to the exercises of previous chapters for help, these images will be in play when you are telling the story and will enhance your voice and body expression. Little by little, as you practice and as your familiarity with the story grows, you will find yourself discovering new opportunities for creativity and enjoyment in the story.

With these ideas and techniques as a starting point, you can analyze and explore the remaining events: the firefly's visit with his relatives, his plunge into the fire, and his desperate attempts to put out the flame burning his body.

How Uncle Rabbit Won Aunt Fox's Heart

Adaptation of Act Two of Uncle Rabbit's Return, *a theatrical text by Daniel Mato inspired by tales of Venezuelan oral tradition.*

Some time ago, ten or twelve years perhaps, the very coquettish Aunt Fox had four suitors at the same time. And you already know who they were: the three strong, ferocious animals of the jungle—Uncle Tiger, Uncle Lion and Uncle Cayman—and the small, astute, and indomitable Uncle Rabbit.

Days and nights went by, and Aunt Fox still had not decided on any one of her three large-sized suitors because as far as Uncle Rabbit was concerned, she didn't take him seriously. She even sympathized with him, saying, "Oh, Uncle Rabbit! How can you want me to fall in love with you, when you are so small and weak ... and on top of everything else, you have such big ears! Everyone would make fun of me, and you couldn't defend me. What's more, you couldn't go out to hunt in order to feed me."

"But Aunt Fox, you're letting yourself be too impressed by the large size of those suitors of yours. The truth is that all three are already under my authority. They're even in my service. I tell you, just between us here and not a word to anyone else, that I use Uncle Tiger as a horse."

"Ha, ha, ha, ha! Oh, Uncle Rabbit! If you have anything going for you, it's that you're so witty and funny. How are you going to ride Uncle Tiger? You seated on Uncle Tiger as if he were a horse? Ha, ha, ha, ha, ha, ha!"

"Fine, if you don't want to believe me, go right ahead."

Uncle Rabbit spoke in such a way as to pique Aunt Fox's curiosity.

"No, it's not just that I don't believe you; no one could believe such a thing. And tell me, might it be, by chance, that Uncle Lion fans you when it's hot?"

"Well, he doesn't fan me because I don't order him to; but when I can't find a good shade tree, I call him and order him to shade me by letting me lie down between his paws."

"Oh, Uncle Rabbit! You are so amusing!"

"Okay, don't believe me if you don't want to, but that's how it is."

With this, Uncle Rabbit half turned to leave. Aunt Fox was suddenly seized with doubt and begged him to forgive her, promising that if he showed her his power over the three large animals, then she would give him her love. Uncle Rabbit accepted the challenge, and he proposed coming to Aunt Fox's house mounted on Uncle Tiger, with a hair from Uncle Lion's beard in one hand and a fang from Uncle Cayman in the other.

This suggestion satisfied Aunt Fox, and she agreed. Filled with hope, Uncle Rabbit said goodbye to Aunt Fox and left by the path that went to the river. On the way, he composed a little poem so that he wouldn't forget what he had promised:

With Uncle Cayman's fang
And the hair of Uncle Lion,
I'll mount that stupid tiger
And Aunt Fox will then be mine.

When Uncle Rabbit came to the banks of the river, he called out, "Uncle Cayman! Yoo-hoo! Uncle Cayman! Hurry! Aunt Fox told me to tell you that she wants to see you."

"Really? I'm coming, I'm coming."

"Hurry, and I'll go ahead to tell her you're on your way."

Uncle Rabbit went a short way and then hid in the bushes on the side of the road. Once there, with a good club in his hands, he waited for Uncle Cayman to pass by. Uncle Rabbit perked up his ears, stretched out his neck, and watched carefully. When Uncle Cayman, who is very slow and awkward when out of water, passed by, he hissed from the bushes, "Psst, psst."

Uncle Cayman turned his head in the direction of the call, opened his mouth, and asked, "Who's calling me?"

At that moment Uncle Rabbit hit him right in the jaw with the club, using such force that one of Uncle Cayman's teeth flew out in the air. Uncle Rabbit, ran, ran, ran … and caught the fang with the dexterity of a great baseball player. Then he scampered away, singing his stanza:

With Uncle Cayman's fang
And the hair of Uncle Lion
I'll mount that stupid tiger
And Aunt Fox will then be mine.

As he went along the road, he almost stumbled into Uncle Lion, who had just finished feasting on a deer and was stretched out under some trees taking a nap. Taking advantage of the fact that Uncle Lion not only wasn't hungry but was practically in a stupor from the heavy meal, Uncle Rabbit came up to him and said:

"Hello, mighty and good-looking friend! How are you?"

"What do you want, Uncle Rabbit? Let me sleep in peace."

"Of course, Your Young Highness … but … ooh, what's this I see! Uncle Lion, how shameful! No one has seen this before?" asked Uncle Rabbit, staring at Uncle Lion's beard.

"What? What's wrong?" said Uncle Lion, raising his head in alarm.

"You have a gray hair in your beard, Your Majesty. How can that be? Imagine what would happen if Aunt Fox saw it."

"Just be quiet, Rabbit, and pull it out. I order you to!"

"Your desire is my command, Your Highness!" said Uncle Rabbit, and after pulling one hair out from Uncle Lion's beard, he started down the road again. Once he was far enough away, he started to sing his little poem and headed for Uncle Tiger's den.

The most complicated matter remained, but Uncle Rabbit's cunning knew no limits. And, besides, his love for Aunt Fox made him ready to do anything. And so, when he got close to the tiger's den, he threw himself down at the foot of a tree and began to complain and cry very loudly. Uncle Tiger lost no time in coming out to see what was happening:

"What's the matter, Uncle Rabbit? Why are you acting like this?"

"Oh, oh, oh, oh, oh!"

"Well, what's the matter?"

"Oh, Uncle Tiger! I ate some weeds, and I can't stand this stomach ache, I can't even walk. Oh, Uncle Tiger, help me! Help me and I promise that I'll never play irritating jokes on you again. Oh, oh, oh, oh! And I promise to help you win Aunt Fox's love. Oh, oh, oh, oh!"

"How could you help me, lowly Rabbit?"

"Oh! I don't know, Uncle Tiger. I promise you that I'll figure something out, but help me."

"Figure it out in a hurry, or instead of helping you, I'll eat you!"

"I've got it! I've got it! Did you know that what Aunt Fox most appreciates is nobility and the desire to serve others?"

"Really?"

"Absolutely. I think that what you should do … No, forget it, forget it, you couldn't do it …"

"Tell me, tell me. Or else I'll eat you!"

"Okay, if you insist so much, I'll tell you. I think that the best way to impress Aunt Fox is … for me to climb up on your back and for you take me to her house so that she can treat my illness."

"Are you crazy? No one climbs up on my back and certainly not for Aunt Fox to see."

"I told you that you couldn't do it. Well, you are lost to Aunt Fox. I only wanted to help you. I'll bet that Uncle Lion is already there. Better to leave me in peace with my illness. Oh, oh, oh, oh!"

"No, no, Uncle Rabbit. Please help me. Climb up on my back. Climb up."

Finally, Uncle Tiger begged. And that is how Uncle Rabbit succeeded in mounting the tiger's back.

When he arrived at Aunt Fox's house seated on Uncle Tiger, Uncle Rabbit raised his arms, showing Aunt Fox the hair from Uncle Lion's beard in one hand and Uncle Cayman's tooth in the other. When Aunt Fox saw all this, she was filled with admiration for her hero. She didn't even look at Uncle Tiger. She ran with arms opened wide to embrace Uncle Rabbit, and she carried him into her burrow.

And so, the small and clever Uncle Rabbit managed once again to play a trick on the three strongest animals of the jungle.

Outline for Telling the Story

Introduction: Some time ago, ten or twelve years perhaps, the coquettish Aunt Fox had four suitors at the same time. They were the three strongest animals of the jungle—Uncle Tiger, Uncle Lion and Uncle Cayman—and the small, but cunning, Uncle Rabbit.

Principal Actions	**Dialogues and/or Complementary Details**
1. Aunt Fox could not decide upon any of the three large animals; she didn't even take Uncle Rabbit into account.	
2. Uncle Rabbit boasted about his power and proposed a way to prove it to Aunt Fox. They agreed that if Uncle Rabbit arrived mounted on Uncle Tiger holding a hair from Uncle Lion's beard and a tooth from Uncle Cayman, then Aunt Fox would give him her love.	
3. Uncle Rabbit went to the river and to lure Uncle Cayman out of the water, told him that Aunt Fox was ordering him to call on her.	
4. Uncle Rabbit went on ahead and hid in the bushes.	
5. When Uncle Cayman passed in front of his hiding place, Uncle Rabbit hit him with a club, and a tooth flew out of Uncle Cayman's mouth. Uncle Rabbit took the tooth and continued on his way.	
6. He found Uncle Lion taking a nap after a big meal.	
7. He went up to Uncle Lion and made him believe that there was a gray hair in his beard.	
8. Uncle Lion asked him to take the gray hair out. Uncle Rabbit removed it.	
9. Throwing himself on the ground near Uncle Tiger's den, Uncle Rabbit complained and cried.	
10. Uncle Tiger came out to see what was happening.	

Principal Actions	**Dialogues and/or Complementary Details**
11. Uncle Rabbit said that he was feeling very sick and promised that he would help Uncle Tiger win Aunt Fox's love in exchange for his help.	
12. He convinced Uncle Tiger that the best way to win her over was for Uncle Rabbit to mount him and be carried to Aunt Fox's house so that she could treat Uncle Rabbit's illness.	
13. Uncle Rabbit climbed up on Uncle Tiger's back.	
14. Uncle Rabbit arrived at Aunt Fox's house mounted on Uncle Tiger, at the same time holding Uncle Cayman's tooth and the hair from Uncle Lion's beard in his hands.	

Ending: When Aunt Fox saw Uncle Rabbit, she was filled with admiration, and she ran to him and took him into her burrow.

Ideas for Telling the Story

Uncle Rabbit stories, which are shared in the most varied of settings, are usually told for no other purpose than to entertain the listeners, especially children, and it is perfectly acceptable that you tell them for that reason, too. I think that as a teller, however, you should know, first, that the story is about a very important character in the history of the art of storytelling, and, second, that Uncle Rabbit stories are associated with fundamental aspects of several contemporary Central and South American cultures and with a distinctive, rich, and animated manner of telling as well.

Uncle Rabbit is the most popular character in the oral traditions of almost all the regions of Venezuela. He is so popular that Uncle Rabbit tales have been recast as children's stories by such prestigious authors as

Filar Almoina de Carrera, Arturo Uslar Pietrihit, and Rafael Rivero Oramas. The latter, in his role as Uncle Nicholas (Tió Nicolás), told the stories on radio for many years. In addition, Uncle Rabbit serves as the point of reference in *Uncle Tiger and Uncle Rabbit*, Antonio Arráiz's portrayal of stereotypes in the Venezuelan society of his time.

But Uncle Rabbit stories are popular far beyond Venezuela. We find this same character in the Uncle Rabbit stories of Costa Rica and Colombia. In Puerto Rico he is called Compae Conejillo, in the Dominican Republic Seño Conejo, in Haiti Compere Lapin, and in the South of the United States Brer Rabbit. His stories are frequently told in Cuba, Ecuador, and Brazil with one or the other of these names. Uncle Rabbit came to the Americas in the memory of African slaves and found fertile soil for development here. Skillful African tellers adapted the old stories to the new surroundings, and in each region the local animals were integrated into the stories as the hero's companions or rivals. Some scholars have attributed the vitality of these stories throughout centuries of slavery and other forms of the subjugation of African cultures precisely to Uncle Rabbit's role as a fictional avenger of the weak. Perhaps this is also why children are so enchanted by his stories, a point that you, as a teller, should reflect on. What is crucial to understand is that Uncle Rabbit is a cunning trickster who always wins out over his generally larger and more powerful enemies by using his astuteness, intelligence, and, perhaps, that same greed that can be found in his rivals.

But, as I said earlier, Uncle Rabbit is associated with a distinctive, rich, and animated manner of telling. I am referring to the various styles of African tellers, many times called *griots*. If you think back to the short passages we dedicated to Africa in our section entitled "World Tour of Storytellers in Action," you will recall that these narrative styles usually include music, dramatization, recitation, singing, the use of masks and other objects, and intense interaction with the audience. I am sure that at this point in the book—that is, in this communicative experience with paper and ink in which you and I are participating—you already suspect that I'm not telling you all these details by chance. I do so because I want to suggest that when you say "Uncle Rabbit," you feel yourself heir to a passion that is centuries long and because I want to recommend that you tell this story in a manner consistent with this rich narrative tradition.

An important feature of this story is that it has five characters in it. When you prepare your adaptation, you should decide if you are going to portray each of them in their respective dialogues. If you want to tell the story but feel that you cannot portray five characters differently, you can opt for depicting only two of them, for example Aunt Fox and Uncle Rabbit. Later, as you become more familiar with the story and develop your personal skills as a teller, you will be able to incorporate other character portrayals. But, one way or another, this story, or rather this narrative tradition, cries out for character portrayal that is exaggerated, to a certain degree even satirical and "overly" energetic.

Whatever your decision, the information given above offers a good point of departure for portraying Uncle Rabbit. You can certainly enhance your portrayal, however, if you note that the well-known twitching of his nose and the quickness of his movement are two almost obvious elements. With regard to the other characters, the same methods of preparation we used for the earlier stories are applicable here: directly observe the characters that you can and learn about the behavior and habits of the rest through encyclopedias and other popular or specialized works. Be sure to note, however, that for all these characters, "Uncle" is part of their name. This designation suggests a very marked humanization; it is no longer simply a case of a rabbit or a tiger, but of Uncle Rabbit and Uncle Tiger.

Another interesting possibility is to make puppets or masks for all or some of the characters and to work with them, beginning with the suggestions and ideas found in Chapter Five. Remember that I'm not proposing that you present the whole story with puppets, but only some or all of the dialogues; in any event you should keep yourself visible to the public. The same could be said about masks.

If you opt for using masks or puppets, I suggest that you consider not using any kind of prop in your portrayal of Uncle Rabbit so that you have the advantage of using different facial expressions to portray how his tricks evolve. You can create a direct relationship between Uncle Rabbit and the members of your audience by resorting to looks of complicity, commenting about the development of the story, or openly asking for ideas about how he can defeat his rivals. The result would be an opportunity to animate and interact with your listeners, and both these techniques are characteristic features of various African styles of storytelling. The song, for example, offers an easy way to encourage audience participation. If you sing it to a well-known melody, the audience could easily accompany you by clapping, or you could even sing it once so that they learn it. Of course, if you play a musical instrument, don't hesitate to incorporate this ability into your telling of the story.

How to Tell Stories: A Latin American Perspective

NOTES

Translator's Note 1: NAPPS, the National Association for the Preservation and Perpetuation of Storytelling, was later renamed the National Storytelling Association. In 1998 it was restructured into two organizations: the National Storytelling Network (NSN) and the International Storytelling Center (ISC). Today NSN reports a membership of some 1,500; this figure includes 200 schools, libraries, and storytelling guilds or organizations. Among other activities, NSN sponsors an annual conference and an award program to recognize tellers for their contributions to the art of storytelling. ISC produces the internationally known National Storytelling Festival, which dates back to 1973 and was the spark that ignited the renaissance of storytelling in the United States. The three-day festival drew an audience of some 10,000 people in 2014. It is one of some 200 annual storytelling festivals in the United States today.

Translator's Note 2: Mato's Spanish version of "Little Red Riding Hood" is taken from Carmen Gaite's translation of the story as it appeared in Bruno Bettelheim *Presenta los Cuentos de Perrault* (Barcelona: Editorial Crítica, 1980). The text presented here draws largely from the Perrault version as rendered in Andrew Lang's *Blue Fairy Book* (first published in 1889) but adds details that are found in Mato's text.

Author's Note: In spite of the style of an "origin myth" that I have deliberately given to the story, it is of my own creation and has no relation to any oral tradition. It is an example of the exercise suggested at the end of Chapter Two concerning the creation of origin myths. On the other hand, the references to the morphological peculiarities of the tree and its relationship to the environment and animal species are based on direct observation and consultation of botanical works. The scientific name of the species is Couroupita guianesis, of the family Lecythiadacedae; it has two common names, "mucurutú" and "taparón." *[Translator's note: In English, it is commonly called the cannonball tree].* This story was expressly created for the purpose of environmental education. However, it can be used for many of the exercises suggested in Part Two.

BIBLIOGRAPHY

1. World Tour of Storytellers in Action

The references cited in the section of Chapter One entitled "World Tour of Storytellers in Action" are from the publications given below. Many of them contain extensive information about different ways of telling stories throughout the world.

Abrahams, Roger. *The Man of Words in the West Indies: Performance and the Emergence of Creole Culture.* Baltimore & London: Baltimore, The J. Hopkins University Press, 1983.

Armellada, Fray Césareo. *Taurón Pantón II. Así Dice el Cuento.* Caracas: Editorial Del Ministerio de Educación, 1964.

Beck, Ervin. "Telling the Tale in Belize." *Journal of American Folklore* 93.370 (1980): 417–434.

Biblioteca Nacional José Martí. *Teoria y Técnica del Arte de Narrar. Colección Textos para Narradores,* 5 vols. Havana: 1966, 1967, 1968, 1973.

Broderman, Miriam. "Algunas Consideraciones sobre el Trabajo Literario con Niños y Jóvenes en Cuba." Paper presented at the Fourth National

Meeting of Promoters of Books for Children and Youth [IV Encuentro Nacional de Animadores del Libro Infantil y Juvenil], Guadalajara, Spain, May 1988.

Córdova, Luis. "Narración Oral 'For Export' o Aventuras de un Cuentacuentos en Argentina." *Imagen*. (Caracas). 100-37 (1988): 33.

Civrieux, Marc de. *Wattunna. Mitología Makiritare*. Caracas: Monte Ávila, 1970.

Colombier, Clair. "¿Qué Cuento Es Ése?" *Parapara: Revista de Literatura Infanta*. (Caracas). No. 12 (1985): 36–39.

"Crean Asociación Nacional de Narradores de Cuentos." *El Excelsior*. (Mexico). Año LXIX, Vol. V, No. 250.008, 15 Nov. 1985, section "La Cultura al Día," 2–3.

Dorson, Richard. "Folktale Performers." *Handbook of American Folklore*. Ed. Richard Dorson. Bloomington: Indiana University Press, 1983.

Herskovits, Melville. *Man and His Works. The Science of Cultural Anthropology*. New York: A.A. Knopf, 1948.

Spanish trans. by M. Hernández Barraso. *El Hombre y Sus Obras*. 3ª ed. Mexico: Fondo de Cultura Económica, 1981.

Hrdlicková, V. "Japanese Professional Storytellers." Ed. Dan Ben-Amos. *Folklore Genres*. Part Two, 171–190. Austin & London: University of Texas Press, 1976.

Jemio, Lucy. *Literatura Oral Aymara* Bachelor's thesis in literature, Department of Humanities and Sciences of Education, Universidad Mayor de San Andrés, La Paz, 1986.

Leon-Portilla, Miguel. "Prefacio" and "Introducción General," *Literatura del México Antiguo: Los Textos en Lengua Nahuatl*. Caracas: Biblioteca Ayacucho, 1978.

Lizot, Jacques. *El Hombre de la Pantorrilla Preñada y Otros Mitos Yanomami*, trans. Victor Fuenmayor. Monograph No.212. Caracas: Fundación La Salle de Ciencias Naturales, 1975.

Malinowski, Bronislaw. *Magic, Science and Religion, and Other Essays*. United States of America: The Free Press, 1948. Spanish transl. by Antonio Pérez Ramos. *Magia, Ciencia, y Religión*. Barcelona: Planetar-Agostini, 1985.

Mato, Daniel. *Cuenteros, Cuentahistorias y Cacheros del Oriente Venezolana*. Barcelona: Edo. Anzoátegui, Fondo Editorial del Caribe, 1993.

_____ *El Arte de Narrar y la Noción de Literatura Oral. Protopanorama Intercultural y Problemas Epistemológicos*. Caracas: Universidad Central de Venezuela, 1990.

_____ "Narración Oral: Fundar un Arte." Rudy Mostacero, ed., *Oralidad en la Literatura y Literatura de la Oralidad*, 50–77. Maturín, Venezuela: Instituto Universitario Pedagógico Experimental, 1985.

_____ "Narradores Afrovenezolanos en Acción." *Revista del Instituto Andino de Artes Populares*. (Quito, Ecuador). 12 (1989): 43–50.

_____ *Narradores en Acción: Problemas Epistemológicos Consideraciones, Teóricas y Observaciones de Campo en Venezuela*. Caracas: Academia Nacional de Historia, 1992.

_____ "Primer Festival de Narración de Cuentos." *Imagen*. (Caracas). 100-28 (March 1987): 37.

Maunas, Delia. "La Vox y el Alma." *Lea*. (Buenos Aires). 28 (1988): 46–49.

NAPPS. *National Directory of Storytelling 1988 Edition*. Jonesborough, 1988.

NUPPO-Núcleo de Pesquisa e Documentacao da Cultura Popular. *I Jornada de Contadores de Estorias da Paraíba*. NUPPO, Universidad Federal da Paraíba, Joao Pessoa, Brasil, 978.

Ortiz, Fernando. *Los Bailes y el Teatro de los Negros en el Folklore de Cuba*. La Habana: Publicaciones del Ministerio de Educación, 1951.

_____ "Se Realiza Taller de Cuenta Cuentos." *Ultima Hora*. (La Paz). Año LX, No. 14 (1 Sept. 1988): 785. Segunda Seccion, Sebillot, Paul. *Contes des Marines*. Paris: G. Charpentier, 1882.

Le Folklore. Litterature Orale et Ethnographie Traditionnelle. Paris: 0. Doin et fils ed., 1913.

Sherzer, Joel. "Strategies in Text and Context. Cuna Caa Kwento." *Journal of American Folklore* 92.364 (1979): 145–163.

Wilbert, Johannes. *Warao Oral Literature*. Caracas: Editorial Sucre, 1964.

Spanish trans. by P.A. Vaquero. *Textos Folklóricos de los Indios Waraos*. Caracas: Mimeo, Fund. La Salle, n.d.

Wilbert J. and K. Simoneau. *Folk Literature of the Mataco Indians*. Los Angeles: University of California, 1982.

Zhenren, Y. "Liu Jinting, Rey de los Cuentistas." *El Correo de la UNESCO*, Año XXXVIII, Agosto 1985, 28–29. Published in Paris.

2. Storytellers on the Art of Storytelling

In addition to the book you have in your hands, there are others on the art of storytelling written by storytellers. The books listed below contain different ideas and practical recommendations, and each of them will enrich your vision of the art of storytelling and will increase your opportunities for developing your expressive and creative skills.

Bryant, Sara C. *How to Tell Stories to Children*. Boston: Houghton-Mifflin, 1905. Reprinted 1973.

Spanish trans. by Ana Ramon de Izquierdo. *El Arte de Contar Cuentos*. Barcelona: Hogar del Libro, 1984.

Cappe, Jeanne. *Expériences dans l'Art de Raconter des Histoires*. Tournai-Paris: Casterman Eds., 1952.

Pastoriza de Etchbarne, Dora. *El Arte de Narrar un Oficio Olvidado*. Buenos Aires: Editorial Guadalupe, 1975.

Pelegrin, Ana. *La Aventura de Oír. Cuentos y Memorias de Tradición Oral*. Madrid: Editorial Cincel, 1982.

Sawyer, Ruth. *The Way of the Storyteller*. New York: Penguin Books, 1987.

3. Books about Dance, Theater, Body Expression, and Oratory and Books with Exercises to Enhance Your Expressive, Creative and Dramatic Potential

Bernardo, Mane. *Títeres y Niños*. Buenos Aires: EUDEBA, 1962.

Boal, Augusto. *Técnicas Latinoamericanas de Teatro Popular (Una Revolución Copernicana al Revés)*. Buenos Aires, Ed. Coregidor, 1975.

_____ *Jeux pour Acteurs et Non-Acteurs. Pratique du Theatre de l'Opprime*. Paris: Éditions François Maspero, 1978.

Spanish trans. by Graciela Schmilchuk. *Teatro del Oprimido/2. Ejercicios para Actores y No Actores*. Mexico: Ed. Nueva Imagen, 1980.

Canuyt, Georges. *La Voz*. Buenos Aires: Librería Hachette, 1982.

Carnegie, Dale. *Public Speaking and Influencing Men in Business*. Kingswood Surrey, U.K.: World's Work, LTD, 1913.

Spanish trans. by Jorge Ciancaglini. *Cómo Hablar Bien en Público e Influir en los Hombres de Negocios*. Buenos Aires: Ed. Sudamericana, 1978.

Cohen, Edwin. *Oral Interpretation*. Chicago-Palo Alto: Science Research Associates, Inc., 1977.

Doat, Jan. *L'Expression Corporelle du Comédien*. Paris: Librairie théatrâle, 1944.

Spanish trans. by Oswaldo Bonet. *La Expresión Corporal del Comediante*. Buenos Aires: EUDEBA, 1976.

Feldenkrais, Moshe. *Awareness through Movement: Health Exercises for Personal Growth*. New York/London: Harper & Row, 1972.

Spanish trans. by Luis Justo. *Autoconciencia por el Movimiento*. Barcelona: Ed. Paidós, 1985.

Fux, María. *Danza, Experiencia de Vida*. Buenos Aires: Ed. Paidós, 1979.

Grotowski, Jerzy. *Towards a Poor Theater*. New York: Simon and Schuster, 1968.

Spanish trans. by Margo Glantz. *Hacia un Teatro Pobre*. Mexico: Ed. Siglo XXI, 1981.

Hethmon, Robert H. *Strasberg at the Actor's Studio*. New York: Viking Press, 1965.

Spanish trans. by Charo Álvarez and Ana M. Gutiérrez C. *El Método del Actor's Studio*. Madrid: Ed. Fundamentos, 1984.

Stanislavski, Constantin. *Rabota Aktiora nad Soboi.*, Chast' I and Chast' II. Moscow: [n.p.], 1937.

English trans. by Elizabeth Reynolds Hapgood. An *Actor Prepares*. New York and London: Routledge, 1964.

Spanish transl. by Salomon Merener. *El Trabajo del Actor sobre Sí Mismo*. Buenos Aires: Ed. Quetzal, 1977.

_____ *Rabota aktiora nad roliu*. Moscow: [n.p.], 1957.

English trans. by Elizabeth Reynolds Hapgood. *Creating a Role.* New York: Theater Art Books, 1961.

Spanish trans. by Salomon Merener. *El Trabajo del Actor sobre Su Papel.* Buenos Aires: Ed. Quetzal, 1988.

Stokoe, Patricia. *Expresión Corporal.* Buenos Aires: Ricordi, 1978.

Expresión Corporal, Arte, Salud y Educación. Buenos Aires: Editorial Humanitas-ICSA, 1987.

4. Promotion of Social and Cultural Programs; Social and Educational Applications of Various Arts; Books Containing Useful Analyses and Ideas for Developing Your Own Applications

Works found in Section Two of the Bibliography, "Storytellers on the Art of Storytelling," contain many ideas for applications, almost all of which are directed toward the field of education, and I highly recommend that you consult them. The following references also offer interesting analyses and, above all, criteria to guide you in your work.

Aguilar, Maria Jose. *Cómo Animar Un Grupo.* Buenos Aires: Instituto de Ciencias Sociales Aplicadas, 1990.

Aretz, Isabel. *Manual del Folklore.* Caracas: Monte Ávila, 1984.

Ander-Egg, Ezequiel. *Metodología y Práctica de la Animación Sociocultural.* Buenos Aires: Editorial Humanitas, 1986.

_____ *La Practica de la Animación Sociocultural.* Buenos Aires: Instituto de Ciencias Sociales Aplicadas, Editorial Humanitas, 1990.

_____ *Repensando la Investigación-Acción-Participativa.* Bilbao: Servicio Central de Publicaciones del Gobierno Vasco, 1990.

Bettelheim, Bruno. *The Uses of Enchantment: The Meaning and Importance of Fairy Tales*. 2nd ed. New York: Knopf, 1977.

Spanish trans. by Silvia Furió. *Psicoanáilisis de los Cuentos de Hadas*. Barcelona: Editorial Crítica, 1979.

Broderman Ortega, Miriam. *Círculos de Interés de Narraciones Infantiles*. La Habana: Editorial Orbe, 1980.

Cervera, Juan. *Cómo Practicar la Dramatización con Niños de 4 a 14 Años*. Madrid: Cincel-Kapelusz, 1981.

Ciari, Bruno. *Le Nuove Tecniche Didattiche*. Rome: Editori Riuniti, 1961.

Spanish trans. by M. Isabel Salvador. *Nuevas técnicas didácticas*. Barcelona: Reforma de la escuela, 1981.

Columbres, Adolfo. *Manual del Promotor Cultural*. 3 vols. Buenos Aires: Editorial Humanitas, 1990.

David, Jose. *Juegos y Trabajo Social*. Buenos Aires: Editorial Humanitas, 1990.

Degh, Linda. "Grimm's *Household Tales* and Its Place in the Household: the Social Relevance of a Controversial Classic." *Western Folklore* 38.2 (1979): 83–103.

Feijoó, María del C. and Sarah Hirschman: *Gente y Cuentos*. Buenos Aires: Estudios CEDES, 1984.

Freinet, Celestin. *Les Techniques Freinet de l'Ecole Moderne*. Paris: A. Colin (Ligugé, impr. Aubin), 1964.

Spanish trans. by Julieta Campos. *Técnicas Freinet de la Escuela Moderna*. Mexico: Siglo XXI, 1979.

Freire, Paolo. *Pedagogía del Oprimido*. Buenos Aires: Siglo XXI, 1974.

Gili, Edgardo and Pacho O'Donnell. *El Juego. Técnicas Lúdicas en Psicoterapia Grupal de Adultos*. Barcelona: Gedisa, 1978.

Heisig, James W. *El Cuento detrás del Cuento*. Buenos Aires: Editorial Guadalupe, 1976.

Herans, Carlos and Enrique Patiño. *Teatro y Escuela*. Barcelona, Editorial Laia, 1982.

Huberman, Hugo y Comunidad de las Escuelas No. 18 y 27. *Cuentos Que Se Cuentan en Lanús*. Buenos Aires: Municipalidad de Lanús, [n.d.].

Lodi, Mario. *C'èsperanza Se Questo Accade al VHD*. Torino: Einaudi, 1972.

    Spanish trans. by Roda M. Pericás. *Crónica pedagógica*. Barcelona: Editorial, Laia, 1974.

Marín Ibañez, Ricardo. *La Creatividad en la Educación*. Buenos Aires: Editorial Kapelusz, 1974.

Mato, Daniel. *Cuentos para Hacer Muchos Cuentos*. Caracas: Editorial María DiMase, 1985.

_____ "Criterios Metodológicos para la Investigación y Reactivación de las Formas Tradicionales del Arte de Narrar." *Folklore Americana* (IPGH-OEA, México) 50 (1990): 141–154.

Movimiento di Cooperazione Educativa. A *Scuola con il Corpo*. 1974.

    Spanish trans. by Xavier Moret. *A la Escuela con el Cuerpo*. Barcelona: Reforma de la Escuela, 1979.

Murcia Florián, Jorge. *Investigar para Cambiar. Un Enfoque sobre Investigación-Acción Participante*. Bogotá: Cooperativa Editorial Magisterio, 1990.

Ndiaye, A. Raphael. "The Problem of Traditional Cultures." *Congress of the IBBY* September (1982): 6–10. Published in Cambridge.

Palermo, Juan Angel. *Didáctica, Narrativa y Recreación del Cuento en la Escuela*. Buenos Aires: A-Z Editora, 1986.

Pamplillo, Gloria. *El Taller de Escritura*. Buenos Aires: Editorial Plus Ultra, 1982. Editorial.

Pardo Belgrano, Ruth, et. al. *Teatro: Arte y Comunicación. Actividades de Clase*. Buenos Aires: Plus Ultra, 1981.

Passatore, Franco, et al. *Io Ero l'Albero (Tu il Cavallo)*. Rimini: Guaraldi, 1972. Published in Spanish as *Yo Soy el Arbol (Tú el Caballo)*. Barcelona: Reforma de la Escuela, 1976.

Pastoriza de Etchebarne, et. al. *Valoración de la Palabra, la Narración sin Láminas*. Buenos Aires: Editorial Guadalupe, 1979.

Pavlovsky, Eduardo. *Reflexiones sobre el Proceso Creador / El Señor Galíndez*. Buenos Aires: Editorial Proteo, 1976.

Peck, Jackie. "Using Storytelling to Promote Language and Literacy." *The Reading Teacher* 43.2 (1989): 138–141.

Puentes de Oyenard, Sylvia. *El Cuento y los Cuentacuentos*. Montevideo: AULI, 1987.

Read, Herbert. *Education through Art*. New York: Pantheon Books, [1974].

Spanish trans. by Luis Fabricant and Ida Germán de Butelman. *Educación por el Arte*. Buenos Aires: Ed. Paidós, 1982.

Rodari, Gianni. *Grammatica della Fantasia*. Torino: Einaudi, 1973.

Spanish trans. by Carlos Alonso and Adela Alos. *Grarnatica de la Fantasia*. Barcelona: Reforma de la Escula, 1979.

_____ *Tante per Giocare*. Rome: Editori Riuniti, 1974.

Spanish trans. by Carmen Santos. *Cuentos para Jugar*. Barcelona: Alfaguara, 1983.

Satz, Antonia. *Las Artes del Lenguaje en la Escuela Elemental*. Buenos Aires: Editorial Kapelusz, 1954.

Sciacca, Giuseppe M. *Il Fanciullo e il Folklore*. Bologna: Malipiero, 1957.

    Spanish trans. by Ricardo Nervi. *El Niño y el Folklore*. Buenos Aires: EUDEBA, 1965.

Schultz de Mantovani, Fryda. *La Torre en Guardia. Lógica del Mito en la Infancia y en los Pueblos*. Buenos Aires: Editorial Plus Ultra, 1978.

Vallón, Claude. *Practique du Théatre pour Enfants*. Lausanne, Paris: P.-M. Favre, 1983.

    Spanish trans'. *Practica del Teatro para Niños*. Barcelona: CEAC, 1984.

Vega, Roberto. *El Teatro en la Educación*. Buenos Aires: Editorial Plus Ultra, 1981.

5. Some Easily Found Collections of Traditional Venezuelan Oral Tales

There are countless collections of traditional Venezuelan oral tales. Many of them, however, have not been in circulation for some time or else were published only in editions of limited circulation. Here are some readily accessible collections that contain valuable material.

Armellada, Fray Cesáreo. *Taurón Pantón*. Caracas: Universidad Catolica Andres Bello, 1973.

Armellada, Fray Cesáreo and C. Bentivenga de Napolitano. *Literaturas Indígenas Venezolanas*. Caracas: Monte Avila, 1980.

Barreto, Daisy and E.E. Mosonyi. *Literatura Guarao*. Caracas: CONAC, [1980?].

Blanco, Luis. *Caliberri-Nae Cudeido. Literatura Jivi*. Caracas: Editorial Tinta, Papel y Vida, 1984.

Salas de Lecuna, Yolanda. *El Cuento Folklórico en Venezuela*. Caracas: Academia Nacional de la Historia, 1985.

Tedesco, Italo. *Literatura Indígena en Venezuela*. Caracas: Editorial Kapelusz Venezolana, 1981.

Villafañe, Javier. *Los Cuentos de Oliva Torres*. Mérida: Universidad de Los Andes, 1978.

6. Traditional Venezuelan Oral Tales: Versions and Recreations for Children

Versions and literary re-creations of numerous traditional oral tales have been written and published specifically for children. Some publications of special interest are given below.

Almoina de Carrera, Pilar. *Había Una Vez ... Veintiséis Cuentos*. Caracas: Editorial Ekaré-Banco del Libro, 1985.

Armellada, Fray Cesáreo. *El Cocuyo y la Mora*, adapted by Kurusa and V. Uribe. Caracas: Editorial Ekaré-Banco del Libro, 1978.

_____ *El Rabipelado Burlado*, adapted by Kurusa and V. Uribe. Caracas: Editorial Ekaré-Banco del Libro, 1978.

_____ *El Tigre y el Rayo*, adapted by Kurusa and V. Uribe. Caracas: Editorial Ekaré-Banco del Libro, 1979.

_____ *El Tigre y el Cangrejo*, adapted by Kurusa and V. Uribe. Caracas: Editorial Ekaré-Banco del Libro, 1985.

Nazoa, Aquiles. *El Chivo, el Perro y los Tigres*. Caracas: Editorial Ekaré-Banco del libro, 1989.

Paz Iguana, Ramón. *El Conejo y el Mapurite*, adapted by V. Uribe. Editorial Ekaré-Banco del Libro, 1979.

_____ *El Burrito y el Tuna*, adapted by Kurusa. Caracas: Editorial Ekare-Banco del Libro, 1981.

La Capa del Morrocoy, adapted by Kurusa. Caracas: Editorial Ekaré-Banco del Libro, 1999.

Pietri, Arturo Uslar. *El Conuco de Tío Conejo*. Caracas: Editorial María Di Mase, 1984.

La Fiesta de Juan Bobo. Caracas: Editorial María Di Mase, 1984.

Rivera Oramas, Rafael. *El Mundo de Tío Conejo*. Caracas: Editorial Ekaré-Banco del Libro, 1973.

El Hojarasquerito del Monte. Caracas: Editorial Ekaré-Banco del Libro, 1981.

La Piedra del Zamuro. Caracas: Editorial Ekaré-Banco del Libro, 1981.

7. Additional Works by the Author on Storytelling

The following works by Dr. Mato are not found in the bibliography of the original publication of the book. They are made available here to provide a more complete listing of relevant research conducted by the author.

Mato, Daniel. "Aportes Teóricos sobre la Noción de 'Literatura Oral.'" *Folklore Americano* (IPGH-Organization of American States). 51 (1991): 53–64.

"Cuenteros Afrovenezolanos en Acción." *Oralidad* (by UNESCO's Regional Office for Culture). 2 (1990): 41–47.

"Cuenteros Andinos: Descripciones de sus Desempeños y Consideraciones Metodológicas." *Folklore Americano* (IPGH-Organization of American States). 58 (1994): 53–66.

"Disputas en la Construcción de Identidades y 'Literaturas Orales' en Comunidades Indígenas de Venezuela: Conflictos entre Narradores y Papel de Investigadores y Editoriales." *Revista de Investigaciones Folklóricas* (Universidad de Buenos Aires). 7 (1992): 40–47.

"El Acto de Narrar y la Noción de 'Literatura Oral'. *Actualidades* (Caracas: Centro de Estudios Latinoamericanos Rómulo Gallegos). 1 (1988): 57–75.

"Interculturalidad en la Constitución y Difusión de la 'Literatura Oral'" *Escritura* (Universidad Central de Venezuela) XV(29) (1990): 59–75.

"La Aproximación Semiótica en la Investigación Intercultural del Arte de Narrar." *Boletín de Linguística* (Escuela de Antropología. Universidad Central de Venezuela). 7 (1991): 128–141.

"La Noción de 'Literatura Oral', Obstáculo Epistemológico para el Estudio del Arte de Narrar." *Anuario 1990* (Fundación Nacional de Etnomusicología y Folklore, Caracas). 1990: 87–100.

"No Sólo Palabras. Aproximación Semiótica al Arte de Narrar." *Comunicación* (Caracas) 67 (1989): 12–22.

"Para una Etnografía de las Formas Escénicas en Latinoamérica." *Gestos* (University of California-Irvine) 5(10) (1990): 29–37.

   Reprinted in *Folklore Americano* (IPGH-Organization of American States) 59 (1998): 145–154.

"Problemas Epistemológicos en las Investigaciones sobre América Latina y el Caribe." *Boletín Americanista* (Universidad de Barcelona, Spain) XXXII.41 (1992): 101–111.

"Problemas Epistemológicos en las Investigaciones sobre América Latina y el Caribe: Oralidad, Escritura y la Noción de Literatura Oral."

Folklore Americano (IPGH-Organization of American States) 55 (1993): 41–51.

"The Art of Storytelling: Field Observations in Venezuela." *Traditional Storytelling Today*. Ed. Margaret Read MacDonald. Chicago-London: Fitzroy Dearborn Publishers, 1999. 528–538.

www.ingramcontent.com/pod-product-compliance
Lightning Source LLC
Chambersburg PA
CBHW072008110526
44592CB00012B/1236